Schleiermacher and Sustainability

COLUMBIA SERIES IN REFORMED THEOLOGY

The Columbia Series in Reformed Theology represents a joint commitment of Columbia Theological Seminary and Westminster John Knox Press to provide theological resources for the church today.

The Reformed tradition has always sought to discern what the living God revealed in Scripture is saying and doing in every new time and situation. Volumes in this series examine significant individuals, events, and issues in the development of this tradition and explore their implications for contemporary Christian faith and life.

This series is addressed to scholars, pastors, and laypersons. The Editorial Board hopes that these volumes will contribute to the continuing reformation of the church.

Editorial Board

Martha Moore-Keish, Columbia Theological Seminary
Charles E. Raynal, Columbia Theological Seminary
Leanne Van Dyk, Columbia Theological Seminary
Amy Plantinga Pauw, Louisville Presbyterian Theological Seminary
Donald K. McKim, retired academic editor, Westminster John Knox Press

†Shirley Guthrie, Columbia Theological Seminary

Columbia Theological Seminary wishes to express its appreciation to the following churches for supporting this joint publishing venture:

Central Presbyterian Church, Atlanta, Georgia
First Presbyterian Church, Franklin, Tennessee
First Presbyterian Church, Nashville, Tennessee
First Presbyterian Church, Quincy, Florida
First Presbyterian Church, Spartanburg, South Carolina
First Presbyterian Church, Tupelo, Mississippi
North Avenue Presbyterian Church, Atlanta, Georgia
Riverside Presbyterian Church, Jacksonville, Florida
Roswell Presbyterian Church, Roswell, Georgia
South Highland Presbyterian Church, Birmingham, Alabama
Spring Hill Presbyterian Church, Mobile, Alabama
St. Simons Island Presbyterian Church, St. Simons Island, Georgia
St. Stephen Presbyterian Church, Fort Worth, Texas
Trinity Presbyterian Church, Atlanta, Georgia
University Presbyterian Church, Chapel Hill, North Carolina

Schleiermacher and Sustainability

A Theology for Ecological Living

SHELLI M. POE

Editor

WESTMINSTER
JOHN KNOX PRESS
LOUISVILLE · KENTUCKY

First edition
Published by Westminster John Knox Press
Louisville, Kentucky

18 19 20 21 22 23 24 25 26 27—10 9 8 7 6 5 4 3 2 1

Quotations from Friedrich Schleiermacher's *Christian Faith: A New Translation and Critical Edition,* © 2016 Terrence N. Tice, Catherine L. Kelsey, and Edwina Lawler, are used by permission of Westminster John Knox Press.

Book and cover design by Drew Stevens

Library of Congress Cataloging-in-Publication Data
Names: Poe, Shelli M., author.
Title: Schleiermacher and sustainability : a theology for ecological living / Shelli M. Poe, editor.
Description: First edition. | Louisville, Kentucky : Westminster John Knox Press, 2018. | Series: Columbia series in reformed theology | Includes bibliographical references and index. |
Identifiers: LCCN 2018012529 (print) | LCCN 2018032512 (ebook) | ISBN 9781611648928 (ebk.) | ISBN 9780664263577 (hbk. : alk. paper) | ISBN 9780664264888 (pbk. : alk. paper)
Subjects: LCSH: Schleiermacher, Friedrich, 1768–1834. | Ecotheology. | Sustainability.
Classification: LCC BX4827.S3 (ebook) | LCC BX4827.S3 P645 2018 (print) | DDC 230/.044092—dc23
LC record available at https://lccn.loc.gov/2018012529

Most Westminster John Knox Press books are available at special quantity discounts when purchased in bulk by corporations, organizations, and special-interest groups. For more information, please e-mail SpecialSales@wjkbooks.com.

For the next generation:
Henry and Maggie; Alison, Samantha, and Bobby IV; Walker
Taylor; Sydney and Maxwell; Gabriel and Bjorn
Wynne and Ben
Frederick and Julian; Casey, Megan, and Ellie; Jake
Calvin and Franklin
Katherine, Michael, and Jon

CONTENTS

ACKNOWLEDGMENTS

This project came into being largely due to the encouragement of Catherine L. Kelsey, who saw the potential for a collaborative endeavor of this sort after the 2014 annual meeting of the American Academy of Religion (AAR), which had climate change as its theme. I am grateful for her support in the early stages of the project. Thanks, as well, to the active participants of the Schleiermacher Unit at the AAR who enthusiastically took up the 2014 invitation to put Schleiermacher's thought into conversation with this significant contemporary issue.

Thank you to my summer 2016 undergraduate assistant, Kelsey Jenee Stone, who provided helpful reader responses to early drafts of each chapter, and whose enthusiasm for eco-justice is inspiring. My gratitude also goes to the Westminster John Knox editorial team for their valuable assistance in producing the volume, and to the editorial board of the Columbia Series in Reformed Theology for supporting its publication.

Finally, I extend a special thanks to each of the contributing authors. The volume takes its current form because of their commitment to collaboration at each stage of the process. I am honored to be counted among the contributing authors and to have had the privilege of working with them over the past few years. A very special thanks to Terry Tice, whose consistent encouragement of Schleiermacher scholarship has been critical to the field.

CONTRIBUTORS

James M. Brandt is professor of historical theology and director of contextual education at Saint Paul School of Theology. He is the author of *All Things New: Reform of Church and Society in Schleiermacher's* Christian Ethics and translator of *Selections from Friedrich Schleiermacher's* Christian Ethics. His current research includes community organizing as a resource for ministry and theology, and spiritual formation in theological education.

Anette I. Hagan is curator of rare book collections at the National Library of Scotland. She is the author of *Eternal Blessedness for All? A Historical-Systematic Examination of Friedrich Schleiermacher's Reinterpretation of Predestination*, and *Urban Scots Dialect Writing*. Her current research looks at Schleiermacher's translations and Prussia's intellectual and social circles.

Shelli M. Poe is assistant professor of religious studies at Millsaps College. She is the author of *Essential Trinitarianism: Schleiermacher as Trinitarian Theologian* and coeditor of *The Key to the Door: Experiences of Early African American Students at the University of Virginia*. Her current research explores the intersection of Schleiermacher's thought and constructive theology.

Terrence N. Tice is emeritus professor of philosophy at the University of Michigan. He is the cotranslator of *Christian Faith: A New Translation and Critical Edition*, coeditor of *Schleiermacher's Influences on American Thought and Religious Life, 1835–1920: Three Volumes*, and author or translator of numerous other books and articles. Currently he is emptying a pipeline full of translative works and is analyzing concepts such as ecotheology, science, love, justice and peace making, and forming interconnections between values, ideologies, and worldviews.

Kevin M. Vander Schel is assistant professor of religious studies at Gonzaga University. He is the author of *Embedded Grace: Christ, History, and the Reign of God in Schleiermacher's Dogmatics* and coeditor of *The Fragility of Consciousness: Faith, Reason, and the Human Good*. His current research focuses on questions of grace and history, theory and method in the academic study of religion, and social and political understandings of sin.

Edward Waggoner is assistant professor of theology in the Sam B. Hulsey Chair in Episcopal Studies at Brite Divinity School. He is the coeditor of *Religious Experience and New Materialism: Movement Matters*. His current research centers on Schleiermacher's theological organicism.

ABBREVIATIONS

§1.1   Proposition 1, subsection 1
CE   Friedrich Schleiermacher. *Selections from Friedrich Schleier-*
              macher's Christian Ethics. Edited and translated by James M.
              Brandt. Louisville, KY: Westminster John Knox Press, 2011.
CF   Friedrich Schleiermacher. *Christian Faith: A New Transla-*
              tion and Critical Edition. 2 vols. Translated by Terrence N.
              Tice, Catherine L. Kelsey, and Edwina Lawler. Edited by
              Catherine L. Kelsey and Terrence N. Tice. Louisville, KY:
              Westminster John Knox Press, 2016.
CG   Friedrich Schleiermacher. *Der christliche Glaube nach den*
              Grundsätzen der evangelischen Kirche im Zusammenhange
              dargestellt, Zweite Auflage (1830/31). Edited by Rolf Schäfer.
              KGA I.13.1. Berlin: Walter de Gruyter, 2003.
KGA   Friedrich Schleiermacher. *Kritische Gesamtausgabe*. Berlin:
              Walter de Gruyter, 1980–.
Peiter   Friedrich Schleiermacher. *Christliche Sittenlehre (Vorlesung*
              im Wintersemester 1826/27). Nach größtenteils unveröffentlich-
              ten Hörernachschriften und nach teilweise unveröffentlichten
              Manuskripten Schleiermachers. Edited by Hermann Peiter.
              Berlin: LIT Verlag, 2010.
Sittenlehre   Friedrich Schleiermacher, *Die christliche Sitte nach den*
              Grundsätzen der evangelischen Kirche im Zusammenhaänge
              dargestellt. Edited by Ludwig Jonas. *Sämmtliche Werke* I:12.
              Berlin: G. Reimer, 1843. [1822–23 Lectures]

INTRODUCTION

Schleiermacher and Sustainability

Shelli M. Poe

Friedrich Schleiermacher stands as a central figure in the origin and development of modern theology: he is one of the first to navigate his way theologically through significant sociopolitical, intellectual, and cultural changes in the Enlightenment and post-Enlightenment eras.[1] This volume suggests further that Schleiermacher's mature theology could serve as a beneficial conversation partner for those who would like to address some of the most pressing issues of our own time. In particular, engaging with Schleiermacher's work could inspire a theological vision that supports and engenders ecologically oriented thought and action. To demonstrate how Schleiermacher's theology could yield such fruit, each chapter of this volume engages with one or more of the classical loci of Christian systematics: ecclesiology and ethics, election and ecumenism, creation, providence, and sin. The authors aim to show that analyses and extensions of these doctrinal touchstones could invigorate a theology for sustainable living in a time of planetary crisis.

The present volume moves deeply and broadly within Schleiermacher's thought in order to allow for evaluation, extension, and application of his theological and ethical vision. Schleiermacher is a conversation partner who tarries with us as we consider what kind of theological commitments might encourage the support of the planet and all of its constituents' well-being. As such, the volume is intended for those who are already convinced that Christians ought to live ecologically and who want to drink deeply from a theological well that could provoke and expand over time. By centering on Schleiermacher's theology, the authors aim to offer a substantive theological vision of one particular form of Christian ecological living. Yet although Schleiermacher's work is situated within a particular strand of Protestant Christianity, the ecological theology it inspires calls for ecumenical conversation and action.

A project of this sort might be puzzling for scholars who are primarily familiar with Schleiermacher's early reception history. In some quarters, he has been touted as a theologian who, following Kant, took a turn toward the subject.[2] No longer concerned with objective understandings of the real subject of theology as revealed in the Bible, some interpreters claim that Schleiermacher, influenced by both the Enlightenment and Romanticism, asks theologians to occupy themselves with individuals' private feelings. Although Schleiermacher went terribly wrong in his development of modern theology, so the story goes, he nevertheless paved the way for the pendulum to swing back into the center: from a premodern naiveté about humanity's ability to know the divine mind on the one side, to an Enlightenment confidence in the human self and a Romantic inward turn on the other side; the pendulum settles back into a newly humbled orthodox reception of divine revelation in the Word as expressed in the person of Christ. Schleiermacher's work, on this common rendering, serves as a caution against going too far with Enlightenment and Romantic ways of thinking.

If this is the interpretation readers have inherited about Schleiermacher's significance within modern Christianity, the approach of the current volume will no doubt provide some pause. How could Schleiermacher's theology be used to engage with a contemporary issue that calls for serious engagement in sociopolitical and economic life when his theology is, allegedly, so insularly focused on the private individual's feelings and experiences? If Christians are to act with resolve on issues of great social importance, it might seem difficult to conceive how a theologian with such a weak theological ethic as Schleiermacher supposedly maintains could advance the conversation.

The cognitive dissonance that the history of Schleiermacher's reception may cause for some readers in this regard helpfully pinpoints a major shift in interpretation that has been picking up steam since the 1980s. A new vanguard of Schleiermacher scholarship reevaluates his work in a different way—as a Protestant theologian who engages with the classical sources of the Christian theological tradition and offers a sophisticated proposal for reconstructing theology after the Enlightenment.[3] While a full argument for reevaluating the once-prevalent interpretation of Schleiermacher's theology outlined above is a topic for another book, the present volume shows how a reconsideration of Schleiermacher's theology could reinvigorate and contribute to a theological discussion that is focused not on individual souls or private feelings but on the social formation of persons in relation to Christ and the Holy Spirit within their earthly home. As persons formed in community, Christians are situated within the broader world and—along with the rest of the planet—face an ecological crisis that requires social action. How could Schleiermacher's thought contribute to establishing planetary living among Christians and with others? Schleiermacher's theology—surprisingly, for some—could have a lot to say about this ethical, social question.

CHAPTER OVERVIEW

Each chapter of the book examines at least one important doctrine. Rather than treating these in isolation, the authors place each doctrine in relation to other theological loci within Schleiermacher's thought and to ecological living in today's world. The authors have also taken care to indicate where each chapter may connect with others. Because of the systematic character of Schleiermacher's thought, each author inevitably circles back to ideas presented in previous chapters.

There are two complementary ways of looking at the arrangement of the present volume's chapters. First, the book has a chiasmus structure: It begins with a description of theological ethics as part of ecclesial *action* and moves toward a discussion of election to blessedness or *redemption* in a religiously plural world. It then centers on the interconnectivity of *creation*, moves back to a discussion of *redemptive* providence, and finally returns to social *action*. In a second organizational structure, the book moves between the inner and outer, dynamically linking various aspects of human life. This dialectic is situated in ecclesiology (inner) and ethics (outer) within chapter 1. Chapter 2 indicates the need for limitations in both theological epistemology (inner) and ecumenism (outer). The interconnectivity of all things is emphasized in chapter 3. A discussion of human agency (inner) in relation to providence (outer) is offered in chapter 4. Chapter 5 focuses on the formation of individual persons (inner) and social action (outer). The result of these two organizational structures, we hope, is a highly integrated and thought-provoking book.

Chapter 1 is focused on Schleiermacher's understanding of the church and ethics. James Brandt introduces some keys for interpreting Schleiermacher's theology, including attention to the way Schleiermacher responds to his intellectual context, and to Schleiermacher's Christology and ecclesiology. Brandt then offers a brief overview of Schleiermacher's life and activity to begin to substantiate the claims that his theology and ethics are deeply connected and are embodied in his activity, not least in the social-political realm. Thereafter, Brandt attends to Schleiermacher's understanding of the nature and life of the church as the community of faith. He demonstrates how Schleiermacher's view of the church as a living organism provides a key resource for Christian responses to the ecological crisis that humanity now faces.

Brandt argues that Schleiermacher understands the church's mission as twofold. First, the church has an inner mission to form a community of persons in communion with God, Christ, and one another. Second, the church has an outer mission to transform the larger society so that wholeness and justice prevail. On this view, the church is a grounded community that lives into the reign of God on earth. Brandt argues that Schleiermacher's understanding of the church's inner and outer activity is the culmination of his theological vision, underlining the teleological drive that the church is to embody for the transformation of the world. On this account, Schleiermacher's vision speaks powerfully to the church's call to respond to the ongoing ecological crisis.

Chapter 2 links ecological concerns with economics, election, and ecumenism. I introduce Schleiermacher's concept of *Naturzusammenhang*, or the interconnected process of nature, in his *Christian Faith*.[4] I argue that this notion could be valuable in the construction of a theology that supports ecological economics. However, for Schleiermacher's theology to be an unambiguous resource for ecological living, I argue that both his claim that the Christian community will eventually be comprehensive in scope and also his appeal to an afterlife as the mechanism for the expansion of Christianity need clarification and reappraisal. I present a vision inspired by Schleiermacher's thought that consistently emphasizes the interconnectivity of created humanity and retains the epistemic limits that Schleiermacher himself put in place in his system of doctrine.

Developing a theme introduced in chapter 1—namely, the relation of church and world—I emphasize the plurality and ecumenism inherent in planetary living, even as Christians inspired by Schleiermacher could maintain belief in the election of all to blessedness. In this way, chapter 2 highlights how Schleiermacher's work could be used as part of an ecumenical project that opens outward toward others. By emphasizing appropriate limitations, diversity, and interdependence, Schleiermacher's theology might be used to support the construction of ecological economics.

Chapters 3 and 4 offer two different accounts of Schleiermacher's intertwined doctrines of creation and preservation. Comparing these interpretations is illuminating as an exercise in ecotheology not least because they illustrate how—whether his theology is understood as offering a form of causal determinism or teleological determinism—his theology could motivate Christian action for planetary living.

Chapter 3 engages with Schleiermacher's doctrine of creation. Ed Waggoner argues that Schleiermacher offers a "theological naturalism" in which Christian doctrines explicate religious experiences as an integral part of the one, natural system of finite existence. Waggoner pays particular attention to Schleiermacher's understanding of the divine activity as nonspatial and nontemporal, and of the world as a system of living forces (*Naturzusammenhang*). He suggests that contemporary ecotheologians could benefit from Schleiermacher's theological naturalism when addressing issues of sustainability. By exploring Schleiermacher's doctrine of divine activity and its implications for other doctrines in systematic thought, along with its implications for changing planetary conditions,

Waggoner claims that contemporary Christians might adopt more eco-logically sustainable activities.

Chapter 4 offers an interpretation of Schleiermacher's notion of divine preservation or providence. Anette Hagan argues that in Schleiermacher's view of divine providence, God's creative agency is a necessary precondi-tion for all activity in the universe. Although Schleiermacher understands divine causality as preserving everything that occurs in time and space, Hagan argues that for him, divine causality does not determine particular finite acts or events that issue from human agency considered in them-selves. Rather, divine determination is teleological and always takes the whole universe as its object. In this way, Schleiermacher's doctrine of providence allows for free human causality. In light of this account of Schleiermacher's doctrine of providence, Hagan provides examples of practical actions that Christians can take toward transforming past human actions to create sustainable habits. This chapter both diverges from and builds on Waggoner's work in the previous chapter by taking up the other side of Schleiermacher's doctrine of creation and turning our attention to ways that the divine causality enables human action.

Chapter 5 focuses on Schleiermacher's theology of sin and the culti-vation of nature. Kevin Vander Schel demonstrates that Schleiermacher's original conception of social sin describes sinfulness as a collective condi-tion that distorts communal human action. Ecological devastation, which is a social evil, is a consequence of social sin. Schleiermacher's *Christian Ethics* describes Spirit-led Christian action that aims to complete the cre-ated world. The cultivation of nature is not, therefore, an isolated task but is identical with the formation of virtuous human living. In this way, Vander Schel argues that Schleiermacher's theology offers significant resources for reimagining distinctively Christian ecological living that supports and promotes life for all. This chapter concludes the main chap-ters of the book by focusing on social sin and the formation of human persons.

Terrence Tice's concluding chapter takes a distinctive tone in compari-son to the previous chapters. Weaving together significant autobiographi-cal narrative since World War II and material from the previous chapters, along with other secular and theological contemporary sources, this senior scholar highlights practical actions for turning around the ongoing global economic and planetary crisis. Although Tice presents his chapter in a distinctively Christian frame, he emphasizes that the green activities that are urgently needed today can be carried out by persons of various religious and secular traditions who similarly care for the planet. Moving from more academic to more colloquial style, Tice urges that—consistent with Schleiermacher's theological outlook—confronting the ecological cri-sis requires participation across societal divisions. By focusing on both theological and secular sources, the conclusion surveys the work completed in the volume and then points outward toward engagement with other thinkers and actors who might come to be engaged in ecological projects.

In an era when ecological devastation threatens the very existence of life as we know it on our planet, the need is great to cultivate practices and habits of thought that may slow down and possibly reverse the damage already done. Schleiermacher's thought, though situated at the turn of the nineteenth century in Protestant Prussia, may well speak to the present moment. Together, the authors of this volume aim to show how Schleiermacher's theology offers a substantive and multifaceted theological perspective that has the potential to weave planetary ways of living and thinking into the fabric of Christian life.

1

SCHLEIERMACHER ON CHURCH AND CHRISTIAN ETHICS

James M. Brandt

The purpose of this volume is to engage Schleiermacher's thought, understand it in some depth, and ask how it might speak in our early-twenty-first-century situation, particularly to matters of planetary crisis and the need to develop ecological living. This chapter explores elements of Schleiermacher's vision—his understanding of the church and of Christian ethics—that are of great importance to his theological program. Here we introduce Schleiermacher's life and thought, and analyze the nature and calling of the Christian community as envisioned by Schleiermacher. We consider the nature of the church as laid out in *Christian Faith* and then give particular attention to Schleiermacher's lectures in *Christian Ethics*. The *Ethics* are of great significance, for it is there that Schleiermacher develops his view of the life and action of the church, how it is to live out its calling or mission. We argue that Schleiermacher provides a theological vision of church with great ethical purchase that can speak to our current situation. This is so because his theological system culminates in ethics with a call to live out faith in church and world.

INTELLECTUAL CONTEXT

Schleiermacher lived in a period of enormous intellectual ferment, and his theology was shaped by and responded to the important currents of the day. It engaged the modern worldview forged by the Enlightenment with its new understandings of philosophy, science, and politics. The Enlightenment valued reason, experience, and utility. It exhibited great confidence in the powers of human reason, faith that a mathematical model of deduction can deliver certainty and universal truth in all realms of human endeavor: scientific, political, religious, and moral. The Enlightenment spirit is a spirit of critical inquiry, and critique is brought to bear against traditional ideas and institutions in church and state.

Enlightenment religion is the natural religion of the deists. Deism's creed includes belief in the existence of a supreme being, moral living as the only true worship, and belief that good will be rewarded and evil punished, in this life or the next. This credo can be summarized as belief in God, morality, and immortality. Such rationalist theology reaches its pinnacle in Immanuel Kant, particularly his thinking in his *Critique of Practical Reason*.[1] The second of his great critiques represents a heightening of the moralization of religion such that "rationally permissible belief structure now explicitly rests on the self-certifying moral experience."[2] The moral sense then leads Kant to postulate human freedom, the existence of God, and the immortality of the soul for, he argues, moral experience can only make sense with the acceptance of these postulates. Deism, and its rationalistic rejection of the supernatural, represents a crucial element of the intellectual context that Schleiermacher engages deeply.

In response to Deism's understanding of religion in terms of reason and morality, Schleiermacher proposes a view of religion based on feeling (*Gefühl*), immediate self-consciousness, an intuitive sense of relation to God and the universe, and the positive religions, particularly Christianity. In this way, he moves away from the Enlightenment. However, he appropriates its spirit of critique, particularly Kant's first critique with its clear sense of reason's limits and its rejection of reason's ability to make metaphysical claims. After Kant, metaphysical claims based on reason are bankrupt and another approach to theology is required. Schleiermacher's genius is to turn to feeling and develop theology that adheres to careful limits about the kinds of claims theology can make. In this way, the critical, discerning spirit of the Enlightenment lives on in Schleiermacher's theological and philosophical project even as he transcends it to something new and distinctive.[3]

Opposed to Deism's rationalism is the supernaturalism of pietism and Protestant orthodoxy, the other main religious options of the day.[4] Schleiermacher was deeply influenced by Moravian pietism. His father, Gottlieb Schleiermacher, experienced a pietist awakening under the influence of the Moravians in 1778, and Friedrich was subsequently schooled by the Moravians for four formative years from 1783 to 1787. Lasting influences of pietism on Schleiermacher include stress on personal conviction, a deep sense of communion with Christ, and formation in faith by means of pious practices. Schleiermacher refers to himself as a "Moravian of a higher order" after his critical turn, his rejection of the supernaturalism that marks both pietism and Protestant orthodoxy. Although Schleiermacher was not as deeply influenced by Protestant orthodoxy as by pietism, he knew the systematic theologies of Protestant orthodox thinkers with their commitment to traditional theology. Schleiermacher's theology remains connected to Protestant orthodoxy in that redemption in Christ remains central and he cites many symbols and creeds, even as he develops his own distinctive understanding of Christ and redemption.

The above sketch of the intellectual currents of the day, particularly the opposition between rationalism and supernaturalism, allows us to identify why Schleiermacher is routinely identified as the founder of modern Protestant theology. His achievement was to provide a new basis and method for doing theology that overcomes the opposition between rationalism and supernaturalism. Schleiermacher's theology can be characterized as a "theology from below," that is, a theology whose touchstone is the present experience of faith. Theology is a descriptive enterprise with a focus on what can be experienced and known in human historical life. Theology is rendered in this-worldly terms, grounded in the experience of faith and attendant to the historical manifestations of the faith. Schleiermacher reconceives the claims of theology in a way that moves beyond the impasse between the supernaturalism of Protestant orthodoxy and pietism and the flat naturalism of Enlightenment theology. The way he transcends previous approaches is evident in his understandings of Christ and the church, doctrinal areas that stand at the very heart of his theology.[5]

KEY DOCTRINES: CHRISTOLOGY AND ECCLESIOLOGY

Schleiermacher's Christology begins not with traditional dogma nor with the New Testament picture of Jesus by itself, but with the contemporary Christian's experience of redemption. Starting with the new form of life that the believer receives in and through the Christian community, Schleiermacher works backward to discern the origin of this new reality. The immediately apparent source of the experience of redemption is the Christian community. The community has a particular history that can be traced back to Pentecost, when the spirit of its founder, Jesus of Nazareth, enlivens people and brings the community into existence. Jesus, made real through his Spirit that lives on in the community, is the crucial historical source of the new life experienced by the believer.

Schleiermacher's method, then, is to consider who Jesus must have been in order to communicate this new and higher life to believers through the medium of the church. He concludes that Jesus must be the possessor of a unique and unblemished consciousness of God. Schleiermacher cannot arrive at an understanding of Christ as the incarnation of the second person of the Trinity as traditionally understood, nor as the Chalcedonian formula has it—"two natures in one person." Such claims are beyond what persons can legitimately know and are fraught with logical difficulties. But as the ultimate source of believers' experience of participation in something beyond themselves, something divine and perfect, Jesus must be perfect in his God-consciousness. He is the completion of the creation of humanity in terms of God-consciousness or relation to God, and the culmination of God's intention for humanity. Jesus is the one remaining "supernatural" element in Schleiermacher's otherwise seamlessly "naturalistic" system. Jesus, the new Adam, is inexplicable in terms of his historical context because he was born into a world of sin. He transcends his context in the sinless perfection of his God-consciousness. However, Christ is not absolutely supernatural because he incarnates what God had intended for humanity from the beginning (and what in theory is possible for any human being—a perfect consciousness of God), but he is relatively supernatural in that he cannot be fully explained by the world that shaped and formed him. Christ the unique and perfect Redeemer remains as theology's foundation. This is theology that moves beyond previous frameworks and yet retains a distinctively Christian identity.

Schleiermacher similarly reconceptualizes the church. The Christian community is neither Protestant orthodoxy's "divinely instituted custodian of infallible truths"[6] nor rationalism's voluntary association of like-minded individuals. Instead the church is a living organism, inspired by God to be sure, but caught up in the flux of social and historical life like every other human movement or institution. This conception of the church as a living organism resonates with New Testament images like the branches of the one true vine or the body of Christ. The church is a true community of persons united by a common spirit that is more than the individuals who make up the community. The church is then the medium through which redemption is made known. The spirit of Jesus, the Holy Spirit, enlivens the community and people are drawn through historical influences into its life and the new sense of communion with God through Christ. On the one hand, this community can be comprehended and analyzed as a human historical reality like any other community; on the other hand, the community bears significance for believers as the place they experience this new life. Even Karl Barth, no friend of Schleiermacher's theology, recognized it as a theology "predominantly and decisively of the Holy Spirit."[7]

The understanding of Christ and church that we have sketched shows how Schleiermacher's thought provides a significant turning point in the history of Protestant theology.

SCHLEIERMACHER'S PRACTICE

In our day, Schleiermacher is widely recognized as the founder of modern theology, as we have indicated above. Before we explore Schleiermacher's vision of the church and Christian ethics, we will also note that there is much to be gained by considering not only his theology but also his actual practice as a pastor, professor, and participant in the movement for social reform. His actual practice goes toward my argument that for Schleiermacher, Christian thought culminates in Christian ethics.

In his own day, Schleiermacher was renowned and revered as a pastor and public figure who made enormous contributions to ecclesial and social life in Berlin, where he served Trinity Church from 1809 until his death in 1834. Evidence of the esteem in which he was held includes the enormous turnout for his funeral procession. Conservative estimates indicate some twenty thousand to thirty thousand people lined the streets to mourn and honor the pastor, professor, and social reformer. Another striking indication of Schleiermacher's popularity is that on four occasions when he was in danger of losing his position or even being banished from Prussia altogether because of his reformist political activity, the orders were not carried out, most likely because of his support from the people. The king and his ministers were reluctant to stir up the masses by publicly punishing a prominent pastor and public figure.

Schleiermacher's time was not only an age of great intellectual ferment; it was also a period of enormous social and political upheaval. This period included the American and French Revolutions and much agitation across the Western world for human rights (especially freedom of assembly and freedom of the press); a turn toward democracy or, in the case of Prussia, at least constitutional monarchy; abolition of the feudal system; and expansion of educational opportunities for commoners. When Prussia suffered humiliating defeat at the hands of Napoléon's armies, Schleiermacher roused the people—both burghers and peasants—to participate in efforts of liberation. This was at the same time an expression of nationalism and of a democratic spirit that the king, Friedrich Wilhelm III, feared. Schleiermacher was a leader in the reform movement in Prussia that flourished from 1807 to 1819 and left an indelible mark on Prussian and German social and political history. The reform movement freed the peasants, reorganized the government in order that locales and common people might have more say in governing, and made public education available to commoners, not only the nobility.[8]

Among Schleiermacher's contributions during this period were serving in the Ministry of the Interior under the reformist prime minister Baron Freiherr vom Stein—contributing to reform of the educational system, playing a leading role in the establishment of the new University of Berlin, editing a reform-minded newspaper, and supporting university student groups advocating for liberal and democratic reforms. Not surprisingly, Schleiermacher was also a leader in church issues with the government, acting against the imposition of a new liturgy on the church by the king.

This resistance to the government went both to Schleiermacher's concerns about the content of the liturgy and to his conviction that the church be autonomous in relation to the state.

Perhaps Schleiermacher's most signal contribution to the reform movement came by means of his role as a leading pastor in Berlin. Prussian clergy of the day were under the ecclesiastic section of the Ministry of the Interior and were expected to follow the dictates of the government and otherwise remain politically quiet. Schleiermacher moved beyond the traditional restraints on members of the clergy and came to a new political consciousness. Robert Bigler credits Schleiermacher with inspiring other clerics to political activity: "As both a stimulator and a prototype, Schleiermacher was primarily responsible for the emergence of the most politically oriented elements of the clergy in the period 1815–1848."[9]

Schleiermacher also exercised influence through his service as pastor of Trinity Church in Berlin, where he was in the pulpit from 1809 until his death in 1834. Until 1822, when the Prussian Union brought Lutheran and Reformed Churches together, Trinity was a *Simultankirche*, a home for both Lutheran and Reformed congregations. The Reformed congregation, served by Schleiermacher, was not part of the parish system, and individuals could affiliate with it by choice. Many were drawn to the congregation by Schleiermacher's charisma as pastor and preacher and his commitment to political reform. So it is that at the congregational level Schleiermacher led a community that provided members with spiritual nurture and formation and was also a bastion of reformist politics. Many of the prominent leaders of the reform movement were members of Trinity Church. Here we see, in practice, Schleiermacher embodied his own vision of the church attending to its inner mission to cultivate faith and its outer mission to contribute to the transformation of society.

We will explore Schleiermacher's theology in more detail below, particularly his understanding of the church and its mission. At this point we pause to note the consistency between his theological understanding and his practice of leadership in church and society. As a theologian, Schleiermacher forged a new theology oriented to life in this world and aiming to address the actual situation of church and society. Part of the theological task is to assess and understand the spirit of the times so a witness can be made that connects with people and moves them to live out their convictions in meaningful ways. As a pastor and leader, Schleiermacher embodied these commitments and acted in his various roles to contribute to a society that moved in the direction of greater equity, access to opportunity, and justice. By attending not only to Schleiermacher's thought but also to his practice, we get a glimpse of the pastor and leader who was so beloved by the people of Berlin.

CHRISTIAN FAITH AND ETHICS

One of the most salient contributions Schleiermacher makes to theology is his orientation to the experiences of faith and the historical character of life and thought. Crucial to his theological program in general and to his *Christian Ethics* in particular is the striking recognition of the historically conditioned character of theology itself. Schleiermacher recognizes, in a way that few before him had, the historical relativity of theology. He claims that Christian teaching "includes only propositions that have validity in the church" at a particular time; universal Christian teaching that is valid for all times and places is impossible.[10] This means that ongoing engagement with and reflection on life in all its diversity is a necessary moment in the work of Christian theology.[11]

Similarly, Schleiermacher asserts that there is no final or fixed way to live out the Christian faith or organize the church. How the church lives out its life must be appropriate to a particular historical location, where it is in time and space. This means that Christian theology must always include descriptive analysis of the situation of church and society and must speak and live in a way that is contextually relevant.

One of the ways that Schleiermacher demonstrates the this-worldly character of his theology is his reflection on eschatology, the "last things." While most traditional theology in his day (and often in our own) has eschatology as its capstone, Schleiermacher reenvisions eschatology and fills it with ecclesial and ethical import, making the life and mission of the church—theology's ethical moment—the climax of his theological vision. Schleiermacher renders the culmination of his theology in this-worldly terms by focusing on how the eschatological notion of the reign of God relates to life in the present.

Schleiermacher's analysis of eschatological themes in *Christian Faith* and in *Christian Ethics* is typical of his revisionist approach to inherited theological tradition. He engages traditional concepts with a depth of analysis that carefully weighs their value and significance. When he comes upon a concept that cannot bear the weight traditionally ascribed to it, Schleiermacher does not jettison the concept but seeks its reinterpretation in a way that makes it credible to critical minds chastened by a recognition of the limits of human understanding. So it is with concepts of "life after death" ("the continuation of personal existence") and the "perfection of the church," the key concepts in his eschatological reflection.[12]

Significant affirmations of traditional eschatological claims are present in the analysis of the *Glaubenslehre* (or *Christian Faith*).[13] Schleiermacher notes that the claims for the church's perfection and the continuation of personal existence after death are grounded in doctrinal loci of utmost importance: doctrines of the Holy Spirit and of Christ. Schleiermacher does not reject these claims outright. Instead he weighs concepts carefully, showing how they fit into the larger theological scheme and assessing their significance.

As to the question of life after death, Schleiermacher allows that it can be claimed that "belief in the continuation of personal existence is bound together with our faith in the Redeemer."[14] However, he also notes that the notion of immortality is beyond our ken and we can conceive no coherent picture of it. Most importantly, he affirms that faith in Jesus as Redeemer is not dependent on immortality or even on Jesus' resurrection. A coherent version of Christian faith can persist nicely without such claims. In this way, traditional claims about life after death are called into question.[15]

However, when it comes to the notion that some are eternally damned, Schleiermacher raises significant reservations. Damnation, or "reprobation," sits uneasily with Christian sympathy for all persons and is inconsistent with God's universal love. Schleiermacher asserts that there exists a milder, universal view, "traces of which are also to be found in scripture, that there will one day be a universal restoration of all human souls resulting from the power of redemption."[16] This universal view, he claims, should be acknowledged alongside traditional views. With the reservations posed about life after death it becomes clear that life beyond the grave is not the culmination of Schleiermacher's theological system. And this nod toward universal salvation moves toward a broader view of salvation. It is certainly a step toward a larger vision of salvation that can encompass the whole of creation and include concern for the wholeness of the natural world.

The second key idea analyzed under eschatology in the *Glaubenslehre* is that of the perfection or consummation (*Vollendung*) of the church. The idea of the church's perfection is affirmed more strongly than the idea of life after death because Christian consciousness knows that the Spirit animates the life of the church. The church lives, grows, and expands in the way that other human societies do, for even the work of the Spirit is "subject to the laws of temporal life."[17] Since the church's growth and expansion are observable, the church's perfection can be imagined. However, Schleiermacher argues that under the conditions of temporal life the church can never be perfected, for the world's opposition can never be overcome in a final way as long as human procreation continues.

The perfection of the church, then, is a most significant eschatological theme in the *Glaubenslehre*, but it is not a doctrine in the strict sense "since our Christian consciousness can have absolutely nothing to say about this state that is completely unknown to us."[18] Schleiermacher asserts that this state is conceivable "under conditions completely unknown to us and only vaguely imaginable."[19] More positively, the church's perfection does have meaning in that it is "always the object of our prayer."[20] It represents "unbroken fellowship of human nature with Christ," a hope to which Christian consciousness looks and a hope that animates Christian activity. So the analysis of the church's perfection in §157 confirms its opening claim: "The representation of [the church's] perfected state is directly useful only as a pattern to which we are to draw near."[21] The real significance of the most important eschatological theme in the *Glaubenslehre*, the perfection of the church, lies in ethics. It provides a vision that motivates the activity of the Christian community.

The notion that the vision of the church's perfection functions as a pattern for current life and activity is striking in its anticipation of the theology of hope of the twentieth century. Seeking to counter critiques that eschatological hope is world-denying and escapist (as it can be), advocates of a theology of hope, such as Wolfhart Pannenberg and Jürgen Moltmann, argue that the vision of the reign of God (Jesus' central message) inspires an active hope; it moves persons and communities to proleptic anticipation of God's reign in the here and now. This notion of eschatological hope inspiring activity in the present world is strikingly similar to Schleiermacher's rendering of eschatology in ways that emphasize its significance for Christian life and activity.

While the central eschatological concept in the *Glaubenslehre* is the perfection of the church, in *Christian Ethics* the reign of God becomes an organizing concept. *Christian Ethics* culminates Schleiermacher's theological system, and with it the reign of God becomes the ideal which inspires the church to action and is the measure of that action.[22]

That Christian ethics is the culmination of the doctrinal system is supported by the way it corresponds to the teleological character of Christian faith. Ethics names the *telos*, the goal toward which Christian action tends. As a teleological religion, Christianity "has a predominant intention toward the moral task . . . In Christianity all pain and all joy are pious only in so far as they are intended for activity in the Reign of God."[23] As Schleiermacher explains, "In light of the teleological character of Christianity we cannot imagine any completely developed pious moment that does not pass over into activity or that does not contribute to activities already in progress in a definite way and combine with them."[24] The theological system culminates in ethics as its crowning moment, just as Christian piety culminates in activity.

The eschatological theme of the reign of God names the highest good that directs all Christian action. For Schleiermacher, the reign of God *is* Christian ethics: "The Reign of God on earth is nothing other than the way of being Christian that must always come to be recognized through actions. The presentation of the idea of the Reign of God on earth is therefore nothing but the presentation of the way for Christians to live and act, and that is Christian ethics."[25]

The reign of God is established by the action of Christ, and all Christian action is to be a continuation of Christ's action. Schleiermacher understands the broadening action of the church in terms of activities which seek to expand the sway of the Christian disposition (formation of the capacities for knowing and willing) and the formation of talent for the sake of disposition. This expansion occurs both within individual persons and to persons who are not yet within the Christian communion. The end point of this process is the "perfection of the whole of the human race in Christ."[26]

Schleiermacher's vision of the reign of God and of Christian ethics may seem anthropocentric, perhaps in a way that could limit its contribution to an ecological vision. However, for Schleiermacher the human person or moral agent is the embodied self, shaped by the natural and cultural world that bears down on it. There is no real Kantian separation between noumena and phenomena, reason and nature, motive and action, even if we make such distinctions in thinking about these matters. Thus Schleiermacher proposes a rich and suggestive understanding of the moral agent as an embodied self existing in a relation of reciprocity with the "world" in which it exists and involved in an ongoing process of formation in which the agent's duty is to act in ways aimed at the highest good.[27] This understanding of the embodied character of human being provides an important warrant that can move toward affirmation of ecological awareness and action in Christian theology.

For Schleiermacher, then, the highest good must encompass the integration and perfection of all goods of human life. Since human life is inextricably bound up with the natural, physical world, attention to ecological concerns is consistent with Schleiermacher's vision, even if it was not at the fore in his own day. The goal of human historical life from the perspective of Christian ethics is life in all its manifestations appropriated and brought together to be in service of the reign of God. God's reign includes the perfection of the Christian disposition in all persons and the perfection of all nature and talent formation. Thus Schleiermacher's *Christian Ethics* points beyond a narrowly anthropological vision. It is a short step for us in the twenty-first century to take Schleiermacher further and assert that the human task and calling include work to preserve and protect nature that it might reflect the glory of God.

The key point here is that Schleiermacher provides a vision of eschatology that is grounded in and oriented toward life in this world, the only world we have. As Eilert Herms points out, Schleiermacher's specification of the reign of God being "on earth" indicates that it has to do with "morality in life that is not yet perfected."[28] The goal of theology is for faith to come to reflexive self-understanding that can inform Christian life in the world. The capstone of theology is the vision of the reign of God, which—extrapolating one step beyond Schleiermacher—we can identify as the completion of all creation. And, with Schleiermacher, we can affirm that the vision of God's reign calls us to act in the present. Here is one way Schleiermacher's understanding of theology can inform a contemporary reflection on faith and ecological living, valorizing the importance of ecological thinking and activity as a claim on Christian life.

THE INNER MISSION OF THE CHURCH

We turn now to a deeper investigation of Schleiermacher's ecclesiology in order to understand its significance in his theological system and to identify the character of the church and its inner and outer mission. The importance of the church in Schleiermacher's theology has often been overlooked because of the way he grounds his theology in an analysis of Christian self-consciousness. This grounding leads some interpreters to identify his theology as "subjectivistic" and "individualistic."[29] Against this, we will argue that Schleiermacher's theological system "rests not so much on 'psychologism' (Brunner) as on a 'sociology of the religious consciousness' (Troeltsch)."[30] Schleiermacher's theology cannot be adequately understood unless its ground in the social character of Christianity is recognized.

The importance of the church is asserted from the very beginning of the *Glaubenslehre* when Schleiermacher identifies dogmatics as a discipline pertaining solely to the Christian church. Theology has both its ground and its goal in the community of faith. Theology arises as reflection on the faith and practice of the church, and its purpose is to gain deep understanding of ecclesial life in its particular context in order to inform the ongoing ministry and leadership of the church.

Schleiermacher understands the centrality of the church as an element of Christian consciousness itself, for redemption includes awareness that it is "grounded in a new, divinely wrought collective life."[31] Not only is this the case, but the church in a union of human and divine is on par with the presence of God in Christ. Schleiermacher says, "We will come to the view that our collective life, equally seen to be something divinely wrought and seen to be something divinely derived from Christ, is wholly one and the same thing."[32] Again, Schleiermacher can assert that "the true manifestation of [Christ's] dignity" is "identical with [Christ's] efficacious action in establishing community."[33] The church as corporate life is the fellowship of believers with Christ such that "Christ is also to be the soul in the particular community, yet each individual is to be the organism through which the soul has an effect."[34] The church as it is considered as a whole and as it is enlivened by the Spirit is the place where communion with Christ is manifest; it is the medium of redemption.

The church as the locus of redemption is evident as Schleiermacher examines it in relation to the doctrine of election and the communication of the Holy Spirit. Election, the doctrine of divine grace as the gift of salvation given unconditionally in Christ, is an important lens for understanding the church. In his discussion of election, Schleiermacher emphasizes the church's "natural" operation; election occurs in history as persons are drawn into the church. Election is not, from this point of view, something hidden from human sight in the mystery of God's decree, formulated from eternity and inaccessible to mortals. Schleiermacher identifies a single divine decree (the goal of which is complete communion of all humans with God), made known in Christ and gradually working itself out in human history. Thus Schleiermacher emphasizes the natural means by which divine election is effected: "What proceeds from the *one* point is only gradually spread out over the entirety of space."[35] Election is manifest in history as the church grows and expands its sway in the world.[36] The other important rubric for understanding the origin of the church is the communication of the Spirit. Schleiermacher emphasizes the Spirit as "the unity of life that is inherent in Christian community, viewed as a moral person."[37] The church is a moral agent willing a particular end, the reign of God.

Christian Faith understands the church as a living organism that grows historically, spreading its life and influence gradually as any human community might. For Schleiermacher, the church is distinct from other human communities in that it is the vine which has its origin in Jesus who manifests God's purpose for the world. In Jesus, the single divine decree for the world begins its fulfillment. The Christian confession is that Jesus manifests God's purpose for the world; thus Schleiermacher also works with the idea that the church is the common life into which all other human communities are destined to pass.[38] As a "moral person" the church is analogous to "what is meant in worldly governance" where individuals are welded together in quest of a common goal.[39] The church is distinct from other such communities because of its relation to God's purpose.

We well might worry about this "high" doctrine of the church playing out in a triumphalistic and imperialistic way. Such concern is legitimate especially in light of the absolutist claims the church has often made and the long history of missionary work entangled with Western colonialism. We should also note, however, that Schleiermacher's theology provides some guard against triumphalism. Very significant in this regard is the historical consciousness with which he infuses theology. He recognizes that no manifestation of the church is perfect although the church does participate in the perfection and divinity of Christ and the Spirit. For Schleiermacher, the church's perfection exists in "an eternal way" and "never in appearance."[40] The appearance of the church is never perfect and is therefore in need of constant betterment, an ongoing reformation. Schleiermacher's understanding of the church acknowledges the need for purification of the church, restoring it to an earlier and better state. Roger Haight in his magisterial three-volume study of ecclesiology assesses Schleiermacher's view of the church quite positively and asserts that his recognition that church structures are both human and divine allows him

> to set up a dialectical relationship between the two forces that in the end constitute church life . . . As a result, one cannot expect to find a pure account or example of the will and purposes of God in the church, but only limited and mixed instantiations of freedom and grace that are played out by human decisions in history.[41]

The result, for Haight, is that we can approach the church "realistically with critical reverence."[42] Schleiermacher builds an important element of self-criticism into his theology—explicitly into his ecclesiology—that can provide a guard against triumphalism and imperialism.[43]

We turn now to Schleiermacher's lectures on Christian ethics, for it is there that he analyzes the life and activity of the church. Schleiermacher structures his analysis of the life of the church by means of a distinction between the inner activity of the church (aimed at the life of the church as a community of faith) and the outer activity (how the church relates to the world, to the larger society in which it exists).

The distinction between inward-directed and outward-directed activity is a helpful heuristic device for analyzing the tasks of the church in building up the community in faith and engaging the larger world that Schleiermacher considers "not yet church." In the lectures on Christian ethics from 1822–23, which form the basis for the Jonas edition of the *Christliche Sittenlehre*, the distinction between the inner and outer spheres is the key structural distinction that gives shape to the work as a whole.[44] As Kevin Vander Schel notes, in the 1826–27 lectures, which provide the basis for the Peiter edition, the inner/outer distinction, especially in relation to broadening action, becomes less significant. In its place, the "operative distinction" is that between disposition cultivation and talent cultivation, each of which contains "inward" and "outward" elements. Vander Schel notes that the disposition/talent distinction corresponds to the doctrinal distinction between regeneration and sanctification and connects with the questions about how the Christian life comes about (regeneration) and how skills and talents for the Christian life are facilitated (sanctification). Still Vander Schel notes that "the material presentation of the 1826–27 treatment largely accords with action 'inside' and 'outside' the church."[45]

For Schleiermacher, distinctions are seen as relative rather than absolute, and this applies to the inner/outer distinction. This distinction can function as a helpful heuristic device to organize our thinking, as it did for Schleiermacher. The relativity of this distinction is highlighted by Roger Haight's analysis of the related distinction between church and world. Haight claims, "Few ecclesiologists in the history of the church formulated the relationship of church to the world with more depth and nuance than Friedrich Schleiermacher."[46] He argues that Schleiermacher understands the world not as that which is outside of the church, but as human nature in its whole extent as not (yet) determined by the Spirit. For Haight this means that Schleiermacher is similar to the Gospel of John in identifying the world as good but also caught up in sin, resisting the effects of Spirit. This also means that the church exists in the world and world is present inside the church. The world refers to the natural and prime matter that is made church by the influence of the Spirit.

Bearing in mind the insights of Vander Schel and Haight, we will make use of the inner/outer distinction to structure our analysis because it enables us to identify and name two poles of ecclesial life that are vital, particularly as we think about our call to ecological understanding and living. There are those persons and communities of faith whose passion for a social justice cause leads them to disregard nurturing faith and the community coming together for specific Christian practices of worship, prayer and meditation, study, and small group meetings. Such practices provide nurture, accountability, and grounding in communion with God, others, and the natural world that can help persons and communities persist in the face of disappointment related to a cause. Such persons need the nurture of the faith community in its inner expression. On the other hand, there are those persons and communities of faith who are turned inward and give no attention to the vocation of seeking justice and peace in the world. Such persons and communities need to hear the call to engagement with the larger world and the way such activity can provide meaning.

Christopher Evans's important analysis of the tradition of theological liberalism in the United States can also offer helpful insight as to why attending to the inner/outer distinction is significant.[47] Theological liberalism, a tradition that traces its origin to Schleiermacher, is hard to define, Evans admits. He characterizes it as a movement that seeks to interpret Christianity in the face of an Enlightenment and post-Enlightenment worldview. Theological liberalism supports critical engagement with the Christian traditions and with contemporary intellectual resources. As resources for theological reflection it takes seriously personal and collective experience and critical analysis of society and affirms open theological inquiry. Evans charts the history of this movement, tracing its ebb and flow in US ecclesial, academic, and social life.

Evans sees theological liberalism at a low ebb in the first decades of the twenty-first century, arguing that evangelical Christian traditions have been more successful than liberals at speaking to the great anxiety and fear so prevalent in the United States. He notes that many people live with fears of losing jobs in an unstable economy, of violence in their neighborhoods, and of globalization that brings windfall to some and desolation to others, including the planet. He argues that liberals today need to continue their commitment to larger social justice issues, including the ecological crisis, and complement that effort "through the centrality of worship, prayer, education, and spiritual discipline" that can address anxiety and fear.[48] Evans is affirming attention to both the inner and outer missions of the church in order that it can fulfill more completely its vocation and speak meaningfully to people in their day-to-day experience. Such a balance between the inner and outer missions of the church corresponds to Schleiermacher's concerns in organizing his *Christian Ethics* along those lines.

For Schleiermacher, the task of dogmatics is to answer the question, "What must be the case, given that the religious self-consciousness, the inner religious sensibility, exists?"[49] The analysis of the church in Schleiermacher's dogmatics indicates that Christian self-consciousness or piety includes an immediate sense of the corporate nature of Christian existence; the church is among the most basic themes of dogmatics for Schleiermacher. For it is by being drawn into the living fellowship of the church that an individual can attain what is distinctively Christian: communion with God through Christ and participation in the ongoing manifestation of God's purpose for the world. The task of dogmatics is didactic description of the Christian reality; an indispensable element of that description is the presentation of the church as an organic, living, purposive whole which stands in unique relation to God and God's goal for the world.

In Schleiermacher's view, Christian ethics addresses the question, "What must come to be out of and by means of religious self-consciousness, given that religious self-consciousness exists?"[50] He sees the church as a living organism, a life process; the *Ethics* describes that process. The *Ethics* receives its structure (in both the inner and outer missions) from the three kinds of action that together constitute the life process of the church: restoring action, broadening action, and presentational action.

The impulse to a restoring or purifying action seeks to restore the consciousness of individual or church when it has gotten off track. The need for such action arises in Christian consciousness from moments in which regression from the rule of the spirit occurs. This is felt as pain, and the spirit or higher self-consciousness responds with an impulse to restore the rule of the spirit. Schleiermacher recognizes that when the individual person is in need of restoration, what is called for is church discipline or education. The church as a whole or the larger ecclesial community may also turn from the rule of spirit; the need then is for betterment of the church, its reform.

As Schleiermacher develops his notion of church discipline or education, that is, the restoration of the individual, he is quite critical of ascetic practices and calls instead for a spiritual "gymnastic"[51]—works of mercy, particularly care of and service to those who are sick and poor. Schleiermacher affirms such practices because they are productive of something positive and because they can work genuine purification of spirit in those doing the service. We might include here action that contributes to ecological wholeness. Action to care for the earth might contribute to individual restoration as well as being positive in itself.

Schleiermacher also provides a lengthy analysis of restoration of the whole or the community that is led by an individual. He cites the Protestant Reformation as the prime example of such an effort to purify the church. He sees the reformer as a servant of the ecclesia, calling for the church to return to itself. One way that an individual reformer can effect restoration is through "self-presentation," manifesting the true common spirit of the church so that its sickness is revealed. Such action that calls the church back to itself has particular salience for global ecological concern. The church needs to reform itself to embrace its call to help heal the earth, and this might be done when individuals set forth ecological commitment.[52]

The second form of action in the inner sphere is broadening action, an action that connotes growth, both as individual Christians grow in their depth of Christian disposition and as those outside the community are brought within it. Broadening action is a central action of the church as, Schleiermacher claims, it both presupposes the existence of community and establishes it.[53] Community is a precondition for such action because the aim of broadening action is to expand the sway of the existing church. The church is established by broadening action because when it is successful further community is created. There is a sense here that the church comes into being through its actions: "The church retains its reality only through that which establishes it—namely through continuous activity."[54] Broadening action of this sort might be reconceived for us to include expanding wholeness and *shalom* beyond the human community to include also the natural order. Here is another way in which Schleiermacher's vision is suggestive for the ecological crisis today.

Ecclesial broadening action has the goal of "the broadening of the Christian disposition and the broadening of all true mental talents for the sake of the disposition."[55] Schleiermacher defines the Christian disposition as love, "including love of Christ and of neighbor—these two cannot be separated."[56] In order for such formation to happen in a way commensurate with its character, the church must exist in a public and open way where there is free exchange of views among all members. Open exchange of this sort enables the church to discern what is genuine progress and what is an unhealthy deviation.[57]

The third form of ecclesial action is presentational action. Such action is based in a sense of blessedness and does not seek outward change but seeks to express an inner state in an outward way; this is Schleiermacher's way of naming what Christian worship is about. The church continues what was begun in Christ, expressing outwardly an inner reality. Schleiermacher says that presentational action and community are "equally original."[58]

> The outward movement of an inner determination of self-consciousness, presentational action, rests upon community and produces community. . . . We immediately transform [the formula "Both are equally original"] into an actual conception when we say, "Presentational action is community itself coming into appearance; thus presentational action is also the means by which community can first become an object of consciousness."[59]

In Schleiermacher's view, then, presentational action and community together constitute Christian reality in its most basic form.

Presentational action or worship is defined as "the totality of all actions through which we present ourselves as organs of God, by means of the divine spirit."[60] Schleiermacher distinguishes between worship in the narrow sense of public, cultic worship, and worship in the broad sense, the manifestation of the Christian spirit in daily life.[61] Both are necessary. Without worship in the broad sense, public worship becomes *opus operatum*; it is reduced to a superstitious work without connection to life. Similarly, without public worship the church fails to come into existence as a faith community and communal life withers.

As concerns the inner life of the church, then, the *Christian Ethics* promotes a vision of the church as a living organism that comes to be through its activity. This is especially evident in its broadening action and presentational actions. These two actions bring the church into being. Broadening action accents growth, expansion in intensive and extensive ways. Presentational action is the community as a whole, and individual members as organic members of the community, representing themselves as organs of God. Restoring action provides for self-correction of individual and community and acknowledges the imperfection that remains in the church. What we have in this vision of the inner life of the church is a rich sense of what it means to be a community of faith that takes its call to manifest and live communion with God in a way that builds up a community. This is a community that knows its purpose and can live it out.

The situation of the global church in the early twenty-first century is markedly different from early-nineteenth-century Prussia, and Schleiermacher would be the first to recognize that the theology and practice of the church must be appropriate to its particular context. This exploration of Schleiermacher's rich vision of the church and its inner life is not meant to be prescriptive—that, too, would violate his commitment to phenomenological description of the church and its life. Instead this analysis is meant to inspire further thought about how the church can be church and to lift up the importance of nurturing the faith and life of the community so that it has energy and direction for its significant calling to make a difference in the natural and cultural world that is its home. Only a church that is grounded in its identity as a recipient of God's favor and grace in Christ and continually formed as a community of nurture and accountability will have the resources to make an effective witness in society and address the pressing issues of environmental crisis. Without being prescriptive, we can affirm that Schleiermacher's sense of the church's inner life can be a significant conversation partner as the church seeks to fulfill its calling.

THE OUTER MISSION OF THE CHURCH

As we noted above, Schleiermacher was an activist in the cause of social and political reform and, as a result, was often at odds with the king and government. He was a leading participant in Prussia's political crises in 1806 and 1819. He inspired the church and the people to political activism in the causes of the liberation of Prussia from Napoléon and then its reform. During the reactionary period that began in 1819, he resisted the "throne and altar" movement of the conservative factions and led resistance to the king's attempts to impose control over church and state.

Now we turn to Schleiermacher's articulation of the church's responsibility in the outer sphere, asking about his theological, theoretical orientation toward the larger society.

In Schleiermacher's view, the church is called to participate in the transformation of the world so that it reflects God's intention for equity, wholeness, and justice. Again the focus is on the reign of God and the call to engage the larger natural and cultural world in transformative ways. The reign of God intends the equality and community of all persons, and this becomes a key criterion in assessing life in the outer sphere. Although Schleiermacher does not directly address issues of ecological concern, the way he analyzes how the church and the individual Christian are to fulfill their calling to engage society can be suggestive for current responses to the pressing need for conversion on ecological matters.

The lectures on Christian ethics during the 1822–23 year organize reflection on the outer sphere using the categories of restoring, broadening, and presentational activity, just as the analysis of the inner sphere had been structured. Schleiermacher recognizes that the outer sphere exists prior to and independently of Christianity; the question is how the church is to relate to the world that is its home and context. Schleiermacher's general answer is that the outer sphere is to be taken up and transformed by the Christian spirit.

Life in the outer sphere comprises three kinds of action, and *Christian Ethics* envisions work for transformation in concrete, particular ways appropriate to each of the three forms. Under the rubric of restoring activity, Schleiermacher attends to issues related to punishment and war. Transformation in this connection is manifest primarily as a prophetic critique of social immorality. Transformation in regard to broadening action takes the form of transvaluation whereby cultural goods come to be seen in their relation to the highest good—the reign of God. In regard to presentational action, the distinctive image is that of the Christian spirit's permeation and modification of the cultural world. As the Christian spirit comes to inspire cultural communities of social and artistic expression, they are transformed from within.

Schleiermacher affirms Christian responsibility to advocate change and provide a check on the power of the rulers. He calls for all individuals to act according to their political position and to contribute their "best insight" (*höchste Berathung*) to reforming tendencies.[62] Schleiermacher calls for Christian engagement in the political process, for involvement in movements that would seek to improve the social order. As Birkner notes, the key presupposition to Schleiermacher's position in this regard is a society in which there is freedom of public communication, in which there is a relation of mutual influence between society as a whole and its individual members.[63] This notion of reciprocity between the individual and society and the call for openness in church and society is explicit in Schleiermacher's consideration of the relation between the individual and the whole, and is presupposed in the analysis of the state's betterment.[64]

Under the rubric of broadening action, the distinctive form of transformation is a transvaluation of cultural goods. Cultural goods are seen in a new way in light of Christian faith. In Schleiermacher's view, Christian ethics has the most affinity with an ethics of the highest good; from the Christian point of view, the highest good is the reign of God. For the

Christian, the valuation of cultural goods is altered, relativized, as they are seen in relation to the reign of God. Cultural goods remain good, but they are subordinated to the highest good and taken up into its service; they are transvalued in light of God's reign.

Broadening action in the outer sphere is action that expands the expression of human spirit in nature. Such action is based on the original identity of spirit and nature and is a manifestation of spirit in nature; nature thereby becomes the organ of spirit. Schleiermacher envisions the broadening process in terms of the complementary aspects of "talent formation" and "nature formation." The former concerns the development of human skills and abilities by means of which the human person is able to form the natural world. The latter concerns that formation of the external, natural world by humans. Thus, broadening action comprises educational and economic activity, both broadly construed. The expression of spirit in nature is accomplished as persons grow in knowledge and ability and as this knowledge and ability are employed in their cultivation and formation of the natural world.

In terms of our concerns for ecological justice, Schleiermacher's vision here may seem unhelpfully anthropocentric. There is merit to that concern. However, it needs to be noted again that Schleiermacher affirms the inseparability of spirit and body so the natural and physical finds affirmation in his vision. And if we were to expand Schleiermacher's vision of the reign of God to include the wholeness of all creation including the natural world, his notion that all actions are to be evaluated in light of God's reign would be quite helpful for our consideration of ecological commitment.

Transformation—as the Christian spirit's infiltration and permeation of cultural communities—finds expression in Schleiermacher's consideration of presentational action in the outer sphere.[65] Its distinctiveness resides in its vision of the Christian moving out into the world of social and artistic expression and transforming it from within by the infusion of Christian spirit. Presentational activity in the outer sphere expresses human self-consciousness of its own nature as embodied spirit, its distinctive role as overseer of the natural world, and its sense that this consciousness and activity are thoroughly corporate.

For Schleiermacher, the Christian moral task in this regard is to "strive to manifest the presentational Christian virtues everywhere in all his social relationships with all individuals and always to work at the same time so that the common feeling in each totality to which he belongs is ever more in agreement with the claims of the Christian principle."[66] This is transformation by infiltration so that communities of the outer sphere can be permeated by the Christian spirit and changed from within. Schleiermacher appeals to Jesus' participation in weddings and banquets and Paul's rules about Christian involvement in idolatrous banquets to argue that Scripture supports participation in the wider culture to effect transformation. Social and artistic representation is not to be avoided, but is to be preserved and ever more Christianized.[67]

CONCLUSION

The transformative impulse of the *Ethics* as it finds distinctive expression in the three forms of action is an important contribution to a theology for ecological living. Schleiermacher calls for the church in its particular locale to discern the reality of the world that is its home and context and to engage that world transformatively. He lifts up the importance of prophetic critique in relation to violence and aggression, and to such particular evils of his day as slavery, dueling, and gambling. He calls for earthly goods to be seen in light of the reign of God and evaluated and valued in that light. Expanding his view of God's reign to include all of creation, we can allow this eschatological concept to speak to ecological concern and inspire appropriate action. And Schleiermacher calls for the Christian spirit of love—for us the love of God, others, and the natural world—to permeate all human and natural life. Schleiermacher's vision of Christian calling in the outer sphere offers much food for thought as we consider the mission of the church in relation to the world beloved of God.

In the theology that we have explored in *Christian Ethics*, as in his practice as pastor, professor, and reformer, Schleiermacher presents himself as a provocative dialogue partner for those who would think and act in ways that promote the wholeness of the natural world. His reorientation of theology to ground it in human historical life, affirm the "here and now," and call for proleptic anticipation of God's reign is a vision that speaks still two hundred years later. Schleiermacher's sense of the church's inner mission—to cultivate a community of faith marked by practices of worship, formation and education, and repentance—provides us with a rich vision of the church springing forth repeatedly as the gift of redemption comes to life in concrete ways. His sense of the church's outer mission—to transform all of life that it might more closely reflect the reign of God's wholeness—is a word that can lift the spirit and move us to action for the sake of the world, not least the natural world.

2

AN ECOLOGICAL *OIKOS*

Economics, Election, and Ecumenism

Shelli M. Poe

The previous chapter introduced Schleiermacher's understanding of Christ and the church, and specifically the ways his theology and ethics might inform ecological thought and action among Christians. In this chapter, I take up three intertwined themes in relation to ecological living: economics, election, and ecumenism.[1] Taking up these themes pushes the discussion further outward, drawing Christians into relation with others. Following Sallie McFague, we note that "the Greek word for house, *oikos*, is the source of our words for economics, ecology, and ecumenical."[2] The "world house," as it were, includes a complicated interplay of economically housed human beings, ecological habitats, and religious homes. McFague contends that because of this interplay, theology may be more closely related to economy, ecology, and ecumenism than is immediately apparent. The goal of this chapter is to examine the ways that these themes may coalesce and reinforce one another within Schleiermacher's thought to create a theology for ecological living.[3]

An assumption of this chapter is that habits of thought that are developed or maintained in one arena of human life can be and often are repeated in other arenas. For example, if one's theology privileges one group of people over another, then one might be likely to privilege one group over another in economic policy as well. Or, if one's theology maintains the total growth of one group of people to the extinction of other groups, then one might be likely to allow the extinction of species within the ecological system. As a third example, if one's theology relies on an otherworldly, individual experience as a means for people to receive salvation, then one might similarly downplay the importance of this-worldly social life in economics and environmental policy. Taking into account the interplay of economy, ecology, and ecumenism, I will argue that while Schleiermacher's theology is remarkably suited for contributing to ecological living among Christians, a few features of his eschatology could be brought more clearly into coherence with ecological economics by further emphasizing his own understanding of the diversity of creation and the constraints of his theological epistemology.

Many Christian thinkers committed to ecumenism and religious pluralism find Schleiermacher's *On Religion* a more tractable resource than his *Christian Faith*. The former text is delivered outside an exclusively Christian context and audience. Schleiermacher therefore makes statements, especially in the Fifth Speech, that point up the value and necessity of a plurality of religions as an outworking of human nature. By focusing in this chapter on Schleiermacher's mature theology rather than *On Religion*, I aim to show that his doctrinal work could also be brought into ecumenical and interreligious conversations as well.

The chapter is divided into three sections, which interpret Schleiermacher's theology and constructively engage it with economics and ecumenism. In the first section, I briefly introduce Schleiermacher's understanding of the *Naturzusammenhang*, or the interconnected process of nature. I suggest that Schleiermacher's understanding of the natural world, including humanity, could positively contribute to ecological economics insofar as it emphasizes the whole of interdependent creation, the limits involved in creaturely life, and organic relations.

In the second section of the chapter, I take account of Schleiermacher's understanding of the divine election of all to blessedness.[4] His doctrine of election reiterates the interdependence, limitations, and organic relations that also characterize Schleiermacher's doctrine of creation, and as such could be fruitful for ecotheologies. However, his doctrine of election also leads to a consideration of the afterlife, which Schleiermacher entertains as a way to account for the redemption of those who die without first having become part of the Christian community. Insofar as the idea of the afterlife could make pivotal an otherworldly, individual experience—turning attention away from the present reign of God and the interdependence of humanity within the *Naturzusammenhang*—it does not seem to cohere with Schleiermacher's otherwise rather seamless contributions to ecological economics. I suggest that a modified version of Schleiermacher's eschatology, which foregrounds epistemic humility about an afterlife, could unambiguously support ecotheologies.

In the third section, I take up Schleiermacher's suggestion that the growth of the Christian community will eventually become total. As he envisions it, a guiding Christian idea is that someday all human beings will become part of the Christian community. Combining the idea of an afterlife with the comprehensive growth of the church, Schleiermacher writes, "All who belong to the human race would, sometime or other, be taken up into community of life with Christ."[5] In addition to the ahistorical nature of this claim, it also privileges the growth of the Christian community without regard for the importance of others as others. A parallel habit of thought within ecology would result in a devastating lack of appreciation for the diversity that is so important to the ecosystem's life. As such,

Schleiermacher's maintenance of Christianity's total growth would seem to be at odds with the production of habits conducive to ecological living. Fortunately, Schleiermacher's own emphasis on the proper bounds of Christian theology and the complexity and diversity of the interconnected process of nature could be used to modify this feature of his thought while constructing a theology for ecological living.

ECOLOGICAL ECONOMICS
AND THE *NATURZUSAMMENHANG*

I begin by outlining ecological economics as opposed to neoclassical economics, aiming to show that Schleiermacher's notion of the *Naturzusammenhang* dovetails with the former rather than the latter. According to McFague, a neoclassical economic model understands humanity as a group of individuals who work together to benefit themselves by optimal usage of natural resources.[6] The focus here is on expanding the economy by privileging those with financial capital. For neoclassical thinkers, McFague writes, "as long as the economy grows, individuals in a society will sooner or later participate in prosperity."[7] The problem is that distributive justice and the optimal scale of the human economy to the planet's economy are externalities: "The issues of who benefits from an economic system and whether the planet can bear the system's burden are not part of neoclassical economics."[8] This model lacks a commitment to distributive justice and an acknowledgment of the appropriate limits of human expansion and domination.

In contrast, an ecological economic model, as McFague describes it, takes the planet as its primary object of concern. It understands the earth "more like an organism or community, that survives and prospers through the interdependence of all its parts, human and non-human."[9] This focus on the interdependence of various parts of creation is meant to emphasize the limited function and scope the parts—including human beings—have in relation to one another. As Rosemary Radford Ruether writes, "Humans are within, not outside of, this self-sustaining ecosystem of the natural world. They can only survive themselves by sustaining it."[10] When the organism is healthy, it survives and thrives. In fact, as McFague notes, its members "work together to provide innumerable free services that none could do alone and that we take for granted."[11] Ecological economics, then, diverges from neoclassical economics in three ways: by expanding its vision from humanity to the planet, by emphasizing the need for each part of the one interdependent organism to properly function within its own limits, and by shifting the focus away from competitive relations and toward symbiotic organic relations.[12]

Schleiermacher's mature theology emphasizes these three features of ecological economics so robustly that, admitting some anachronism and exaggeration, we might arguably call him an ecological theologian before his time.[13] First, Schleiermacher's theology has an expansive vision, taking into account not only humanity but the entirety of creation. He invites his readers to imagine "the creation of the world and, along with this, the entirety of the interconnectedness of nature to be *one* divine act."[14] For him, everything is determined as one organic, interconnected, natural process.[15] Under such a conception, each part of creation fits together with the other parts so that "all could just as well be for the purpose of each part, just as each part could be so for all."[16] The divine intention, for Schleiermacher, is set upon the one process of nature and upon its parts insofar as they are included within the whole.[17] Further, recognition of the universe as an interconnected process of nature goes hand in hand with the Christian's sense that everything as a whole depends upon God.[18] In fact, these two fully coincide: "the fullest conviction that everything is completely conditioned by and grounded in the totality of the interconnected process of nature and the inner surety regarding the absolute dependence of all that is finite on God."[19] In this way, Schleiermacher's theology marries an expansive vision of the scope of divine activity with the absolute dependence of the created whole upon God.

Second, Schleiermacher's thought emphasizes the need for each part of the one interdependent organism to properly function within its own limits. Most pertinent to the present discussion, humanity must live within certain constraints. Some of these are imposed by the laws of nature that govern all creaturely life. As Schleiermacher writes, not only human bodies but also objective human consciousnesses are "conditioned and determined by the interconnected process of nature."[20] In the *Dialectic*, Schleiermacher writes, "The idea of the world also determines the boundaries of our knowing. We are bound to the earth. All operations of thinking, even the entire system of our concept forming must be grounded therein."[21] Further constraints are set in place by other human beings. Indeed, human nature itself is constituted interdependently, with reference to each instance of human being.[22] Schleiermacher explains, "If in an individual being within the given species something showed itself that would contradict the earlier definition of the species, then the species would have been wrongly defined all along, and it would have to be defined differently. Or, on the other hand, the identity of the given individual being would simply be mistaken."[23] In this way, the whole of human nature is defined with reference to each individual human being, and the inverse is also true: each constituent of human nature is always understood in relation to the whole. As Schleiermacher writes, personal self-consciousness includes human "species-consciousness" (*Gattungsbewußtsein*).[24] In other words, consciousness of oneself includes consciousness of the whole of humanity. Accordingly, the reality of the *Naturzusammenhang* grounds a coreferential and coconstituted understanding of oneself and humanity within creation. This way of understanding humanity brings to the fore Schleiermacher's heavy emphasis on interdependence within the created sphere, and the limits within which creatures operate and understand themselves.

Third, Schleiermacher's theology emphasizes organic relations. He presents the world and humanity within it as an organic whole because of his understanding of Christ's relation to humanity within creation. For Schleiermacher, all of humanity and the whole of creation is shaped or determined by Christ as one organic whole. He explains, "Christ had come to be determined in the way he was only because and insofar as the whole given interconnection of things was also determined in a certain fashion, and, in reverse, the whole given interconnection of things would have been determined in the way it was only because and insofar as Christ too would have been determined in a certain fashion."[25] Despite the apparent mutuality between the determination of Christ and the world implied in this passage, priority is given to Christ insofar as his person revises the definition of the human species. Schleiermacher writes:

> The creation of human being is first completed in Christ. This is the case, since what is his most inner core distinguishes him from all others; then the being of God dwelling in Christ has to relate to human nature taken as a whole in the same way as the prior innermost core of being a human being related to the human organism taken as a whole. This analogy has already run through the entire presentation up to now, though not explicitly articulated.[26]

For Schleiermacher, humanity's creation is completed by the union of the divine essence with human nature in Christ's person.[27] Because of the interdependent—coconstitutional and coreferential—nature of humanity within the natural world, Schleiermacher goes so far as to say that "Christ was also always coming into being, even as a human person, at the same time as the world was coming into being."[28] This passage brings the organic relation of Christ, humanity, and the whole of creation to its height. We can see here that Schleiermacher's understanding of the *Naturzusammenhang* combines the three features of ecological economics that McFague highlights: an expansive vision of the divine activity that broadens one's view from an insular focus on humanity to the wideness of creation, an understanding of the interdependence of each of the limited parts within the whole of creation, and an organic conception of the relations between human persons and the world we call home.

ELECTION TO BLESSEDNESS
AND PERSONAL IMMORTALITY

Moving now to a consideration of Schleiermacher's understanding of election, I present the doctrine as it appears in his *Christian Faith*, highlighting its emphasis on interdependence, the limits involved in a person's election to blessedness, and the organic relation of Christ with the election of individuals and the whole.[29] After detailing these features of the doctrine of election, I then suggest that a portion of his eschatology, which is connected to the doctrine of election, may need modification in order to safeguard the ecological economic model that his doctrine of creation and theological anthropology otherwise could support unambiguously. The aspect of Schleiermacher's eschatology that may require modification is his suggestion that individual persons might receive redemption in an afterlife. Returning to the distinction between neoclassical economics and ecological economics introduced in the previous section, we can see that this feature of his theology could cohere with a habit of thought similar to that of a neoclassical economic model. A parallel may be identified between the concept of an individual reception of salvation after death and an eventual trickle down of economic benefits distributed to the economy's members. Both of these ideas encourage the development of a privileged portion of society—Christians, in the one case, and those with financial capital, in the other case—leaving to the future the benefits such development may have for others. To avoid this parallel habit of thought, I offer an interpretive and constructive proposal regarding Schleiermacher's system of doctrine that aims to bring his brief focus on the ahistorical individual in his eschatology into line with his overall emphasis on the *Naturzusammenhang* as an interdependent organic whole. We begin with his doctrine of election.

Schleiermacher maintains that there is *"one* divine predestination to blessedness."[30] The divine election of all to share in the blessedness of Christ, however, is not "atomistic," focusing "on the individual as such."[31] "A proper view of the matter," Schleiermacher writes, "cannot possibly arise from such a restriction."[32] Rather, he maintains that there can be no unconditional election of individuals as such because of the mutual conditioning of all individuals, which we have already highlighted.[33] Individuals cannot be absolutely elected to blessedness, since they limit and interact with one another in their election. They are, therefore, relatively elected to blessedness; only the whole of creation is absolutely elected to blessedness.[34] It is important to notice that this move is parallel to Schleiermacher's understanding of the distinction between partial and universal causes: divine causality is that on which the whole depends, whereas individual, partial, natural causes are interdependent within creation.

Keeping in mind this distinction between the absolute or unconditioned and the relative or conditioned, Schleiermacher states that there can be "only *one* unconditioned decree—that is, one by which the whole, viewed in its undivided interconnectedness, exists in the way it does by virtue of the divine good pleasure."[35] Schleiermacher explains:

> Wherever we conceive an aggregate of natural causality as complete in itself and refer to its foundation in divine causality we would be able to assign no basis of determination for the latter other than the divine good pleasure. Now, just as the entire world is ordered by God in such a way that God could say "it is all good," that is, in accordance with God's good pleasure, but in this respect no particular is to be divorced from its interconnection with all the rest, so too if we consider the reign of God as a whole that is complete in itself, we can say only that it is determined as it is solely by the divine good pleasure. That being the case, everything that belongs to Christ's being as he is, on the one hand, and the entire internal multiplicity of the human race in time and space, from which multiplicity the reign of God is formed through Christ, being as it is, on the other hand, are both determined by the divine good pleasure.[36]

In this passage, Schleiermacher highlights the interdependence of the individual and the rest of creation. He also places Christ and the church in the midst of the divine determination of creation and humanity in time and space. The origin of all these things—the natural world, humanity, and the reign of God through Christ—is simply the divine good pleasure. In short, things are as they are because of divine wisdom in carrying out God's unconditional love of the entire world.

The divine election of all to blessedness is, according to Schleiermacher, to be carried out through Christ's organic influence in the church. Sarah Coakley notes that Ernst Troeltsch took "the conception of the Church as an 'organism' with a 'radiation from some strong nodal point,' i.e., Christ, as Schleiermacher's contribution to ecclesiology."[37] By emphasizing the church as the means by which the influence of Christ expands over time, Schleiermacher's theology remains this-worldly in his understanding of the Christian reception of redemption. Redemption does not occur in a flash within the individual human heart, unconditioned by history, tradition, family, friends, and the rest of the matrix of existence. Rather, for Schleiermacher, redemption is received organically in and through the created world's processes, being conditioned spatiotemporally, historically, and through community. Both the election to blessedness and the way in which that election is actualized are bound up with the organic, corporate, or social nature of being human.[38]

Schleiermacher's relational understanding of humanity, or species-consciousness, is so thoroughgoing that he finds it unbearable to think of a portion of humanity as entirely separated from the rest. To think of humanity as separated into an elect portion and a nonelect portion would rend humanity's species-consciousness in two, and thereby stand in tension with the Christian love of neighbor. He explains:

> The shared feeling of Christians is at ease with one or another person's being taken up into the community of redemption earlier or later; however, an irresolvable dissonance does remain if, on the presupposition that there is a continuing existence after death, we were to think of a portion of the human race as entirely excluded from this community. . . . All this gains a whole other perspective, as soon as we hold ourselves to be justified in assuming that this contrast is simply in process of vanishing at every particular point, with the result that everyone who is now still outside this blessed community would at some time or other be within it, deeply touched by the workings of divine grace. This would be the case, for at that point there would be no bifurcation in our species-consciousness anymore, and for that consciousness the merely gradual transition of individuals into the full enjoyment of redemption would be entirely the same as the gradual progress of sanctification is for our personally oriented self-consciousness. That is, it would simply be the natural form that divine activity would of necessity take on in its historical appearance, and, as was stated above, it would be the indispensable condition of all temporal efficacious action of the Word-become-flesh.[39]

While Christians could tolerate the gradual union of all of humanity within the blessedness of Christ, Schleiermacher holds that they could not tolerate a permanent division within humanity.[40]

A problem arises, for Schleiermacher, when a recognition that not all people are brought within the Christian community before death is added to his species-consciousness and to his understanding of the church as the means by which election to blessedness is actualized. The fact that not all people become Christian before they die seems to rend humanity into two groups: those who receive redemption through Christ and those who do not. Thinking of humanity as fundamentally divided into two separated groups would not only disrupt humanity's species-consciousness. It would also call into question the divine government of the world as one whole that is elected to blessedness in Christ and shaped in relation to Christ's Spirit in the church.

Since this division would disrupt Christian blessedness and species-consciousness, Schleiermacher entertains the possibility of an afterlife. He claims that if one were to assume an afterlife, "the condition one would have at death would at that point be simply an intermediate one."[41] In an afterlife, he surmises, God could bring all individuals into the reception of grace. Schleiermacher relies upon the concept of an afterlife as a way to work out how to retain his understanding of divine government and human species-consciousness in light of the fact that many people clearly die apart from the Christian community. By doing so, he retains divine omnipotence and omnibenevolence while avoiding divine arbitrariness and failure.

Although the afterlife might seem to solve these would-be theological problems, by making this move, Schleiermacher uncharacteristically emphasizes the individual and does so in a relatively nonhistorical way. Neither of these moves are particularly beneficial to the ecotheologian. Here we find an entrance of individuals into redemption after death, apart from their historical locations.[42] Schleiermacher himself notes the danger of ahistorical thinking here, when he cautions against imagining how immortality could include survival of the personality after death. Any such imaginative picture, he writes, "can all too easily become detrimental to Christian faith and life and can thus ruin the present for us."[43] As we have seen in chapter 1, Schleiermacher elsewhere takes pains to uphold the historical, social conditions of human life and to emphasize the significance of the present life for Christian faith.

Yet Schleiermacher makes room for a conception of the afterlife within his *Christian Faith*—even though it presents a real danger of spoiling Christians for the present life—in part because of Christ's sayings about his "return or reunion with his own."[44] These sayings seem to imply Christ's personal survival of death, even though "we never do find a cohesive, irrefutable treatment of these subjects anywhere, one that undeniably underlies an aim of imparting firm information concerning them."[45] Because of this lack of a clear treatment of personal immortality, Schleiermacher writes that if the authenticity of Jesus' sayings about his return to his people were called into question by exegesis or were figuratively interpreted, then "faith in Christ as it has been presented here would certainly remain possible."[46] Significantly, Schleiermacher is indicating that a belief in the afterlife is not a pervasive or logical requirement of the system of doctrine he constructs in his *Christian Faith*. For Schleiermacher, Christians could embrace the essential features of Christianity "even if we would have had no intimation of a state after death."[47]

More to the point, then, Schleiermacher maintains that there is only one basis upon which a belief in the afterlife could legitimately arise: the unchanging union of the divine essence with human nature in the person of Christ. Without this, a belief in the persistence of human personality after death "could not find any place within our account of Christian faith-doctrine."[48] The idea of the afterlife, therefore, is just one way of dealing with the dissonance between humanity's species-consciousness, the divine election of all to blessedness, and the fact that the Christian community is not equal to the total human population.[49]

Although Schleiermacher's system does not logically require a conception of the afterlife, he includes this idea because its denial would result in "a thoroughgoing transformation of Christianity" as it is understood in the general populace.[50] As he observes, there is a "generally predominant presupposition within the Christian church of a personal existence after death."[51] As those familiar with Schleiermacher's work know, he is not averse to reconstructing popular understandings of Christian faith and espousing doctrines that would be considered heterodox by the general populace.[52] Nonetheless, here he leaves room for the predominant presupposition of the church as he knows it.

The result is that although Schleiermacher's thought usually emphasizes humanity's interconnectivity within the process of nature, his doctrine of election at this point exhibits two uncharacteristic features: it seems to treat the non-Christian (1) as an individual, (2) whose personal formation in community must be upended by an after-death transformation, which would be a nonhistorical process in the sense that it would occur outside of the time-space matrix with which humanity is currently familiar. There is no doubt that Schleiermacher tends toward such an uncharacteristic claim—ironically perhaps—because of his deep affirmation of Christian love in community, which motivates his account of human personal- and species-consciousness. Even so, the result is an affirmation of the possibility of redemption after death apart from the life humanity currently experiences. Because the transformation of the non-Christian person after death would occur outside the historical life of faith, Schleiermacher's organic, interdependent understanding of humanity curiously drops out of view.

While this may be regrettable in the quest for a theology for ecological living, Daniel Pedersen argues that a reconstruction of Schleiermacher's system of doctrine that excludes the afterlife is not possible without doing irreparable damage to that system.[53] Pedersen argues that given the existence of non-Christians at their deaths, on Schleiermacher's doctrinal system, an afterlife would be required for Christ to redeem the whole world. Since Schleiermacher's theology rests on redemption by Christ, "what is in question in Schleiermacher's account of eternal life is actually the validity of his dogmatics as a whole."[54] Pedersen is certainly correct that Schleiermacher seems to rely on the idea of an afterlife in his *Christian Faith* as the way to ensure universal redemption. As an argument against those who do not recognize the role of the afterlife and universal salvation in Schleiermacher's thought, Pedersen's contribution is significant.[55]

However, his conclusion that the afterlife is logically necessary to Schleiermacher's doctrinal system seems to be unwarranted. Schleiermacher could have avoided an uncharacteristically ahistorical and individual affirmation of the reception of redemption in an afterlife, without doing detriment to the coherence of *Christian Faith*. There is an alternative way to cope with the "irresolvable dissonance" Schleiermacher identifies between the existence of non-Christian persons and the divine election of all to blessedness. Using Schleiermacher's concept of the *Naturzusammenhang* and his characteristic concern for upholding Christian epistemic limits, theologians inspired by him may retain his understanding of redemption within an interdependent created matrix while avoiding reliance on the afterlife for maintaining the universality of the divine election to blessedness.

When constructing that modified position, however, one feature of Schleiermacher's thought that may not be altered is his maintenance of the persistent union of Christ with human nature. As we have already noted, this persistent union is an integral part of his system of doctrine. Without it, there is no redemption. Indeed, this is what Schleiermacher calls the "high-priestly dignity of Christ," that "God sees all human beings only in Christ."[56] Schleiermacher's doctrinal system requires that as long as human nature exists, the person of Christ must be united to it.

It is important to notice, however, that because of Schleiermacher's organic understanding of humanity, this requirement of his doctrinal system seems already to have been met by the life of Christ and his personal "dignity" as the founder of the Christian church itself, without any mention of the afterlife. Each human being is united with Christ and his church organically, just as they are connected with every other human throughout history. The important difference is that—from a Christian perspective—history itself is determined in relation to Christ by divine wisdom. Based on Schleiermacher's organic understanding of creation, it seems that human nature is and always will be united to Christ because of the divine determination of the world in relation to Christ, along with the actual existence of Christ within the one human organism.[57] As part of the organic whole of the *Naturzusammenhang*, which God has shaped in relation to Christ, humanity is already permanently united with Christ. Consistent with the focus of Schleiermacher's theology in general, the incarnation is the key to salvation.

Beginning with this recognition, one resource for developing a this-worldly, organic solution to the "irresolvable dissonance" Schleiermacher identifies may be found in his own discussion of the church's belief in the return of Christ, which has been briefly introduced above. We now take a closer look at Schleiermacher's treatment of this first prophetic doctrine. He notes that the disciples interpreted Jesus' sayings about his return literally. In fact,

> not once could the question be raised among Christians as to whether all of these discourses could perchance designate that future return of

Christ in a way not to be understood in a literal fashion. Hence, . . . the opinion was very quickly established and given currency almost everywhere that Christ's return would coincide with the end of the earth in its present state.[58]

Schleiermacher himself, however, suspects that the sayings in question regarding Christ's return should be taken figuratively rather than literally. Further, he states that "if we bracket out such literal interpretation, then we have no more biblical warrant for the view that reunion of the faithful with Christ . . . depends on such a personal return of Christ."[59] If Schleiermacher would tend to interpret Christ's sayings about his return in a nonliteral way, such that Christ's return is understood as his influence in the common Spirit of the church, then Schleiermacher's thought could likewise tend toward understanding the personal persistence of other human beings after their deaths in terms of their continuing influence in and among others still living. According to Schleiermacher, humanity continues to be united with Christ after the Redeemer's departure from the community in the Spirit of the church. He writes, "The community of the faithful with one another and that of each Christian with Christ are indeed simply one and the same thing."[60] Given this identity, the communion of human persons with deceased loved ones could likewise "be the same thing" as the communion of human persons with those who carry on the spirit of their deceased loved ones—usually, family members and close friends. No literal return of Christ or personal immortality of other humans need be maintained in order to hold the persistent union of Christ with Christians, or deceased persons with family and friends.

Following this train of thought, those inspired by Schleiermacher's theology could affirm the persistent union of Christ with human nature considered as one organic whole without also maintaining that non-Christian individuals would need to receive redemption during a personal survival of death. The persistent union of Christ with human nature could be upheld, first, by acknowledging the existence of Christ along with the interconnectedness of all creaturely existence; and second, by interpreting the persistent union of persons with others as a communion of personal influence and personal formation.

This alternative solution to the "irresolvable dissonance" Schleiermacher identifies, it seems to me, would be more consonant with his epistemic humility regarding things outside human experience and his corporate understanding of the doctrine of election than the notions of individual personal immortality and redemption after death for non-Christians. For Schleiermacher, individuals are elected to blessedness only as part of the whole of humanity. There is no divine election of individuals considered in themselves apart from the whole.[61] Rather, each human being is elected to blessedness only insofar as each is a part of the organic whole. While it may be the case, then, that many individual human persons do not affirm their relation to God in Christ, a theology inspired by the one Schleiermacher constructs in his *Christian Faith* could nevertheless maintain that non-Christian persons' election to blessedness remains a fact of their existence as part of the one human organism. In other words, humanity as a whole—and each individual human in relation to the whole—is organically related to Christ and his Spirit by the divine good pleasure. Thus, Christ's persistent union with humanity and the election of all to blessedness could be maintained without recourse to a notion of personal immortality by which non-Christians could enter the Christian community one by one after their deaths. Moreover, this solution to the "irresolvable dissonance" need not be taken as a form of "anonymous Christianity" *à la* Karl Rahner, as I will demonstrate in the next section.

THE CONSUMMATION OF THE CHURCH
AND ECUMENICAL THEOLOGY

Not having emphasized this alternate way of solving the "irresolvable dissonance" Schleiermacher identifies, his understanding of the one divine decree of all to blessedness and the relation of God in Christ to the *Naturzusammenhang* led him to assert that the Christian community will become total. Returning once more to the distinction between the neoclassical and ecological economic models outlined in the first section of the chapter, a parallel attitude may be identified between this kind of totalizing claim about the Christian community and the neoclassical economic model's disregard for the optimal scale of the human economy within the planet's economy.[62] In neither case is there a recognition that limits might need to be set in place that would preserve others as others to ensure the flourishing of the whole. If Schleiermacher's work is to be an unambiguous theological support for ecological economics, in addition to the modification of an individualized salvation after death as the means to that totalization, his dogmatics requires careful consideration, clarification, and modification in terms of the eventual totalization of Christianity.[63] In the rest of this chapter, I briefly introduce Schleiermacher's understanding of the consummation of the church and aim to bring his totalizing claim about the Christian community into line with his pervasive acknowledgment of the Christian's epistemic limitations and the importance of diversity. My goal in this final section of the chapter is to develop one aspect of a Schleiermacher-inspired ecumenical theology that would be unambiguously coherent with ecological living.[64]

In connection with his doctrine of election, Schleiermacher discusses the consummation of the church. Keeping the interconnectivity of the *Naturzusammenhang* in mind and recalling the historical broadening of the church introduced in the previous chapter, it should come as no surprise that Schleiermacher sees Christ's activity as expanding across the whole of humanity.[65] As we have seen, for him, the corporate completion of humanity's creation comes about through Christ's influence in the church and the world. Moving further, Schleiermacher claims that as the influence of Christ continues through time, "all other communities of faith are destined to pass over into Christianity."[66] In other words, the influence of Christ's person and work will ramify outward through time and space by the divine Spirit in the church until all are brought within the Christian community of grace.

It is important to remember, however, that strictly speaking, "no doctrine of the church's consummation can arise for us, since our Christian self-consciousness flatly cannot say anything about this situation, which for us is entirely unfamiliar."[67] While Christians maintain a belief in the "community that human nature shares with Christ," the consummation of the church—wherein all faiths would pass over into Christianity—would be under "entirely unfamiliar and only waveringly imaginable conditions," that is, in an afterlife.[68] Although the consummation of the church remains a logical possibility, Schleiermacher thinks that Christians cannot actually conceive of the Christian community becoming the only community of faith because they cannot forget that "human procreation does not cease as this course proceeds and sin unfolds anew in each generation."[69] Because of the ongoing development of each new generation, which is influenced by history and sin, the church could not become all in all within history. As such, Schleiermacher writes, "the church cannot attain its consummation within the course of human life on the earth."[70] That being the case, the idea of the church's consummation "is immediately useful only as a pattern that we are to approximate."[71] For Schleiermacher, the consummation of the church is a state that Christians may pray for,[72] but it is not realizable under the conditions of creation. The prophetic idea of the consummation of the church, then, "has never made any claim to producing knowledge in the proper sense but is meant to give shape in a stimulating fashion only to principles already acknowledged."[73] Schleiermacher describes the consummation of the church only after a recognition of these limitations of the concept, as well as the concept's limited use in theology.

Even so, similar to Schleiermacher's comments about an afterlife, we find here two features of this thought that would prove difficult within a theology for ecological living. First, there is some ahistorical thinking involved in his description of the consummation of the church.

Schleiermacher himself recognizes as much when he states that such consummation would be "possible only by a leap."[74] This leap, he acknowledges, seems to make "superfluous the entirety of redemption, attached to community of life with Christ as redemption is."[75] As such, the idea of the consummation of the church tends toward the mythical, or "a historical presentation of something suprahistorical."[76] Second, Schleiermacher's comments on the consummation of the church in his *Christian Faith* also betray a lack of appreciation for religious diversity. If the church is to become total, engulfing and thereby bringing to nothing other religious communities, there is clearly a lack of appreciation here for limits on the scope of the Christian community within the *Naturzusammenhang*.

One way to make Schleiermacher's thought more tractable to ecological theology with regard to the consummation of the church is to highlight the self-prescribed proper boundaries of Christian theology within his system of doctrine. Schleiermacher's theology is not built upon a doctrine of creation or anthropology that is unconnected to the person and work of Jesus of Nazareth.[77] Rather, "within Christianity everything is referred to the redemption accomplished through Jesus of Nazareth."[78] For Schleiermacher, Christian claims arise out of piety in relation to the Redeemer. This means that Christians do not have unfiltered epistemic access to divine activity. Their understanding of divine activity is mediated through Christ. As such, Schleiermacher's *Christian Faith* is clearly focused on the *Christian* community: their religious dispositions, beliefs, emotions, and activities. Christians, because they are Christians, understand the divine government of the world in relation to Christ and his Spirit in the church. A Christian understanding of the divine wisdom in determining the *Naturzusammenhang* and the reign of God on earth, however, need not be supplemented by an additional claim that the Christian understanding of divine wisdom is exhaustive and exclusive. Christians do claim, from their own perspective, that Christ is the exclusive redeemer. From a Christian perspective, as Schleiermacher understands it, there is no other redeemer than Christ. However, the idea that one could survey all religious and secular traditions and decide—from above the fray—that Christianity is the only fully accurate account of divine wisdom would be quite another claim to make. It is the difference between offering one's own perspective and declaring that one knows that one's perspective is entirely and exclusively correct. Schleiermacher would resist making the latter claim insofar as he denies human persons' epistemological ability to break through from—using Kantian language—the phenomenal to the noumenal realm.

As such, Schleiermacher's theology seems to neither entail nor provide warrant for any positive statements about those who are not Christian other than that they are included in humanity, which is elected to blessedness as one organism in relation to Christ. Indeed, Schleiermacher states:

> From our standpoint, the term "passing over" is the most suitable one, because it says "no" to only a distinct action. It is not as if no divine activity, or no divine decree for that matter, would have been implicated in relation to them. Rather, only as a consequence of the overall divine ordering of things is this divine activity so completely bound up in remote internal and external preparations that they merely seem to us to be passed over. . . . Of those who do not evidence these workings we have no basis for declaring anything else but precisely this negation, and indeed only in their relation to the reign of God at a given time and the workings of grace that proceed from it.[79]

A theology inspired by Schleiermacher of the sort I am suggesting, then, would indicate that an appropriate Christian profession with regard to those who are not Christian is ignorance. One might affirm that those who are not Christian are part of the divine ordering of the universe and that they stand in relation to the divine activity and decree of blessedness as an object of the divine good pleasure. Beyond such a statement, however, Christians can maintain nothing other than this: "They merely seem to us to be passed over."

This recognition of Christian epistemic limits could go hand in hand with a robust sense of the natural and historical diversity—including religious diversity—that is needed for the interdependent whole to function.[80] In the introduction to his *Christian Faith*, most of Schleiermacher's comments that relate Christianity to other religions do so in analytical rather than strictly historical terms. He also makes a number of quite regrettable statements, to say the least, about Christianity's relation to other religions.[81] Nonetheless, he acknowledges that Jesus was born into a Jewish context[82] and claims that "Christ could hardly have been a complete human being if his personal existence had not been determined by characteristics of his people."[83] Even though Schleiermacher usually minimizes Jesus' Jewishness, he does recognize that it is in and through Jesus' Jewish body, land, people, and culture that he receives the activity of the divine and acts accordingly.[84] Thus, although Schleiermacher makes a number of ecumenical blunders, he nonetheless recognizes the historical character of religions and their relation to one another.[85] As Thomas Reynolds explains, "Schleiermacher does not regard the religions as incommensurate and self-enclosed historical monads, each utterly relative to its own context. . . . History is an open field of direct engagement between differences, differences that modify each other. Schleiermacher admits as much. There is no solitary community of discourse insulated from the experience of other communities and their modes of discourse."[86]

Going further than this descriptive analysis, Schleiermacher himself recognizes the importance of religious multiplicity. In fact, he maintains that acceptance of religious variety is distinctively Christian:

> Faith in Christ is itself nothing other than the shared sentiment regarding this divine good pleasure in Christ and the holiness grounded in him. Moreover, the consciousness of divine grace, or the peace of God, in the redeemed person is also nothing other than precisely this resting in the divine good pleasure, with respect to the ordering by which the redeemed person has actually been taken up into the domain of redemption.
>   Now, in the world in general we encounter the most manifold gradation of life, from the lowest and most incomplete forms to the most advanced and accomplished forms. Moreover, there can be no doubt that precisely this multiplicity, viewed as the most abundant possible fulfillment in time and space, is the object of divine good pleasure. Furthermore, such gradations do also arise within the domain of human nature. Accordingly, we would likewise reasonably expect within the spiritual domain of life that would have emerged through redemption to find everything that lies between the most meager level and the most advanced level, and we would also view this whole profusion of all that is bound to vital community as the object of the divine good pleasure and would desire to rest in it.[87]

According to Schleiermacher, then, Christians may have peace about spiritual variety precisely because of faith in Christ. As he writes in *On Religion*, "Just as nothing is more irreligious than to demand uniformity in humanity generally, so nothing is more unchristian than to seek uniformity in religion."[88] Although Schleiermacher evaluates religious variety as more or less perfect insofar as it conforms to the Spirit of Christ, the abundance of religious life could also be celebrated as a result of the divine good pleasure in creating and governing the world. In other words, an acknowledgment of the many and plentiful religious traditions and interreligious encounters in human history could form the beginning of an appreciation of religious others as others on whom each historically depends.[89]

In these ways, Schleiermacher's theology could be interpreted as consistent with the notion that all of creation is interdependent both as an ecological whole and as a diverse set of religious traditions.[90] Further, by emphasizing the proper bounds of Christian theology more consistently, and by further highlighting the importance of diversity within religious life in the historically interdependent world, Schleiermacher's theology could be modified to exclude a totalizing claim about the Christian community, a claim that could cultivate an attitude about scale and domination that could feed into a neoclassical economic model. By highlighting the goodness of the *Naturzusammenhang* in all its variety, the divine wisdom in governing the world, and Christian epistemic limitations regarding the precise way in which redemption occurs for those who are not Christian, Schleiermacher's interpreters may affirm that humanity's blessedness might, in fact, be experienced more diversely than Christians know in their own limited community.

CONCLUSION

Ecotheological readers of Schleiermacher might emphasize his concept of the *Naturzusammenhang* and his own recognition that the combination of the notions of the afterlife and the consummation of the church "and their relation to each other does not yield a firmly demarcated, genuinely graphic intimation, nor can such a graphic intimation of either feature be developed out of allusions found in Scripture."[91] By doing so, Schleiermacher's theology could be interpreted and constructively modified to unambiguously support ecological economics. As I have shown, such an interpretation would foreground Christian agnosticism about the method of redemption for those who are not Christian while emphasizing diversity as an essential part of the *Naturzusammenhang*. It would thereby put into question Schleiermacher's prophetic doctrine regarding the Christian communion in relation to other religious traditions, while retaining his focus on the connection of all to Christ through the incarnation and Spirit of Christ within the *Naturzusammenhang*, and his insistence that all are within the scope of divine election. On this account, Christians might claim that the completion of humanity's creation-redemption comes about in the world through Christ's historical and living influence in the church, but they ought to also leave room for Christian ignorance about those who "merely seem to us to be passed over." For Schleiermacher, Christians see the world in relation to Christ and can see it no other way. Yet it is precisely because of this epistemic limitation that they lack a basis for making positive claims about those who are not Christian except that they, too, are elected to blessedness and are within the scope of divine love and wisdom.

In this chapter, we have been considering a confluence of multiple theological loci as they relate to ecology, including economy, election, and ecumenism. Schleiermacher's focus on the *Naturzusammenhang* makes his theological work a valuable resource for those concerned with ecological living. It highlights creaturely interdependence, the limits of creaturely life, and organic relations in ways that could significantly contribute to ecotheologies. After clarifying and reconstructing a portion of his theology, which he, too, has serious doubts about—by removing the afterlife and the totalizing growth of the Christian community within the larger whole of humanity—his mature work could unambiguously support the establishment of sustainable and just planetary living, both economically and ecumenically.

3

SCHLEIERMACHER'S THEOLOGICAL NATURALISM

Critical Resources from His Views about Creation for Contemporary Ecotheologies

Edward Waggoner

> If then my Christian feeling is conscious of a divine spirit within me, which is something other than my reason, I never want to give up seeking this in the deepest depths of the nature of the soul; and if my Christian feeling becomes conscious of a Son of God, who is distinguished from the best of us in a different way from being a "better still," then I never want to stop seeking the generation of the Son of God in the deepest depths of Nature.
>
> —Friedrich Schleiermacher[1]

My task in this chapter is to explore how Schleiermacher's views about creation (i.e., his views about the relationship between divine activity and the world's origin, structure, and dynamism) could be helpful to ecotheologians. When Schleiermacher testified to his Christian experience and to the experience of others in his Christian community, he strove to explain as much of that experience as possible by appealing to the best of what he and his colleagues knew about the world and about themselves as products of the world. I contend that contemporary ecotheologians could critically modify Schleiermacher's theological naturalism and take it in new directions to address issues of sustainability.

I present my case in three steps. In the first, I provide a brief overview of what I am calling Schleiermacher's theological naturalism. I show how Schleiermacher arrived at the premise that divine activity does not occur in time or space, and how he constructed his claims about the world's beginning, the person of Christ, and divine wisdom and love to cohere with that rule. In a second step, I analyze Schleiermacher's view that the world is a system of living forces. In a third and final part of this chapter, I suggest ways for ecotheologians to activate Schleiermacher's theological naturalism for the construction of theological proposals of their own.

A THEOLOGICAL NATURALISM

In his letter to Jacobi, quoted above, Schleiermacher refers to two specifically Christian experiences. He became conscious, he says, of a divine spirit in him that was not the same thing as his reason, and conscious also of a Son of God who was superior, in some way, to the best of other persons. In his major theological work, *Christian Faith* (1st ed., 1821–22; 2nd ed., 1830–31), Schleiermacher takes these two aspects of his personal religious experience to be something common to the religious experience of all Christians. He conceived the task of dogmatic theology to be to articulate such experience conceptually and systematically—that is, to present what Christians ought to say about God, the world, and themselves, on the basis of their shared experiences.

One of the most distinctive features of Schleiermacher's presentation is his commitment to elucidate Christian religious experience as truly "natural." As he explains to Jacobi, he looked for the divine spirit "in the deepest depths of the nature of [his] soul" and for the appearing of a Son of God as "a production . . . in the deepest depths of Nature." Schleiermacher firmly believed that every event in nature (including human being) is completely determined by what precedes it in time and space.[2] He sought to explicate Christian experience as an integral part of the one, natural system of finite existence. For that reason, I take Schleiermacher's system of doctrine to constitute a "theological naturalism." The two features of Schleiermacher's theological naturalism that I find most interesting and potentially helpful for contemporary ecotheologies are his claim that divine activity does not occur in time or space and his belief that the world is a system of living forces.

DIVINE ACTIVITY IN ECOLOGICALLY PERILOUS TIMES

The human species is now a planet-changing force, in ways that we are likely to regret. We have contributed to the extinction of a massive number of species. We cultivate, extract, exchange, and transmute Earth's resources at rates that are pushing Earth's system beyond its current equilibrium, even as our population continues to climb. We have altered the planet's surface, air, and water enough to trigger global climate changes that may prove catastrophic to many forms of life on earth, including our own. Our species must consume less, and consume differently,[3] in order to have any credible hope of ameliorating the climate effects that we have already set in motion. We must adopt habits that are more ecologically sustainable.

That is easier pledged than done. "Sustainability" is a complex, con-tested concept.[4] We cannot hope to flourish if our overall patterns remain unchanged, yet we learn quickly that decisions about the environment, the economy, and equity are morally fraught. After millennia in which humans have exploited one another along intersecting lines of socially constructed identities, we (individuals, corporations, communities, and nations) contribute to unsustainable practices with significantly different intensities, and we have widely divergent capacities to authorize, finance, adopt, and implement new ecological policies. As we strive to live more sustainably, to ask how God might act to help us seems wise.

The first thing that Schleiermacher wishes his readers to understand about divine activity is this: it never occurs in time or space. Were we to posit temporality or spatiality to divine activity, we would abrogate what Schleiermacher calls "the feeling of absolute dependence." Schleiermacher asserts that all Christian religious experience presupposes a preconcep-tual, immediate "feeling of absolute dependence."[5] This feeling lies—as it were—behind all language; but when we express it in words, we may describe it as an awareness that "our entire self-initiated activity . . . issues from elsewhere."[6] Schleiermacher reasons that no finite thing could be the source of our feeling of absolute dependence. To a greater or lesser degree, we influence all finite things with which we interact. We cannot feel our-selves to be absolutely dependent on them. Only a source that is not at all determined by others in time and space could be the source of our feeling of absolute dependence. That source, we call "God." Divine activity does not occur in time or space.[7]

Because any dogmatic proposition that contravenes this premise about divine activity is ipso facto incommensurate with Christian religious experience (on Schleiermacher's view), Schleiermacher accords the prem-ise a formal status as a "canon" within his system of doctrine.[8] By the term "canon" he signals that he intends to apply it consistently: he avoids mak-ing any claim in the system's formal propositions that explicitly or implic-itly conflicts with the rule that divine activity does not occur in time or space, and, naturally, he also avoids explicating his propositions in ways that conflict with it. Schleiermacher succeeded in applying this canon con-sistently. We can see the impact of the prohibition against spatiotemporal divine activity by looking specifically at Schleiermacher's remarks about creation, the person of Christ, and divine wisdom and love.

Schleiermacher's first concern in his doctrine of creation is to insist that nothing whatsoever "is excluded from having been originated by God."[9] Schleiermacher was reluctant to talk about the beginning of finite existence at all, for the reason that humans have "no self-consciousness of a beginning of being."[10] Schleiermacher's second concern is to make perfectly clear that Christians ought not to tell creation stories in which God seems to be subject to the contrasts that characterize finite existence. God's creative activity must not be "defined after the manner of human activity" or by implication "become a temporal activity."[11]

Schleiermacher follows his own guidelines exactly as he continues to explain his views about creation. He does not rely on extended analogies to human actors, such as artists, monarchs, or parents, to convey any of his points. He avoids using titles for God that one commonly finds in theological discussions about God's creating the world, such as Creator (*Schöpfer*), Maker (*Erschaffer*), or Author (Originator) (*Urheber*). He uses some of these titles elsewhere in his system of doctrine, but sparingly, and without any extended, analogical reasoning that could further encourage his readers to think of God's creative activity in overtly temporal or spatial ways.

Schleiermacher's strictures rule out several kinds of creation stories that are popular in Christian theology. For example, Schleiermacher would reject doctrines of creation that depict the source of all finite being as a divine artist (e.g., architect, builder, poet),[12] householder, sovereign covenant maker,[13] gracious self-communicator,[14] conversation partner,[15] or parent.[16] All such root metaphors for God imply that divine activity is subject to the same contrasts that mark finite activity. Though popular, these metaphors are too anthropomorphic to cohere with Schleiermacher's doctrinal system.

By rejecting these anthropomorphic descriptions of God, Schleiermacher forfeits the advantages that theologians working under different rules might gain from them. That is not an insignificant cost. Each of the divine titles mentioned above might signal something about who God and creatures (including the earth itself) are in relation to one another. Many theologians believe that theological stories that feature these particular identities can shape what Christians expect of God and themselves. They are stories that many Christians use to interpret events, characterize challenges, and imagine possible responses to them.[17]

For example, through creation stories about God the Artist, ecotheologians might encourage Christians to imagine the earth itself and all its denizen species and every one of its elements as a beautiful and rare work of divine art. Theologians could suggest, further, that the human species or the dynamic processes that comprise the Earth system or even the planet itself are analogues to an artist's self-portrait. Or perhaps the fundamental constituents of reality (be they matter or energy or something else) mirror the divine artist's own vitality. Ecotheologians could then describe the relationship between God and creatures in aesthetic terms: the divine artist treasures its creation, infuses it with semiautonomous creative powers, and expects humans to relate to themselves and others and the planet in trust, by treating all of it together as God's good, beautiful, unsubstitutable, and life-engendering work of art.

Using this root metaphor of God the Creator as Artist, ecotheologians could interpret human failure to live in ecologically sustainable ways as an indifference to the divine artistry that shows in, through, or *as* the world, or as a misvaluation of particular aspects of God's creative work, or as wanton lust to possess it, or as a radical, existential resentment against it, or even, sadly, as a will to mar and destroy divine art. Ecotheologians who address issues of sustainability using the root metaphor of God as Artist could stress the beauty of each aspect of creation, exhort us to value the planet and all that is in it as an integrated work of art, stress the Artist's ability to repair or reshape that art, and encourage Christians to approach questions of environment, economy, and equity with gratitude for their God-given capacities to connect humans and nonhumans and places and earth in beautiful ways.

Alternatively, by appealing to God's triune life, ecotheologians might interpret human failure to live in ecologically sustainable ways as a resistance to interdependence as such, or an unwillingness to affirm and engage human differences, or as speciesism. A doctrine about God's inner life—the communion of divine persons—could contribute to a sense of human responsibility for other humans, for nonhuman life, for the elements of the earth, or for the planet itself. Promises from the Gospel of John about divine indwelling and home making could ground encouragements to address the interplay of environment, economy, and equity in local contexts. Ecotheologians might suggest practices of prayer that explore the (Pauline) Spirit's capacity to hear and express the groans of creation to the Father in the name of the Son. They might emphasize Jesus' promise that the Spirit would guide believers into truth and suggest that the Trinity, as the distinction-in-relational-unity source of all that exists, has both the power and the faithfulness to bring all creatures to a future in which they can flourish. By insisting that divine activity is never temporal or spatial, Schleiermacher rules out any such approaches.

At first glance, Schleiermacher seems to make a christological exception to his rule. In his remarks about the divine in the "person" of Christ, Schleiermacher employs a fair amount of spatial language. For example, he is willing to speak of "God's becoming human in [the] consciousness [of Jesus]"[18]—which he calls the "being of God in [Christ]" and "a true being of God in him."[19]

However, when Schleiermacher elaborates on this spatial language, he interprets it nonspatially. The phrase "a being of God in him" does not carry any meaning-content other than the claim that Jesus had an uninterrupted, unbroken awareness of the absolute dependence of all things on

God. Schleiermacher implies this when he says that "to attribute an absolutely strong God-consciousness to Christ and to ascribe to him a being of God in him are entirely one and the same thing." He implies a nonspatial understanding again of the idea when he says that there is "an actual being of God" in Christ "inasmuch as we posit God-consciousness in his self-consciousness as determining every element of his life steadily and exclusively."[20]

In subsequent remarks about the union of divine and human in Christ, Schleiermacher provides a clearer report. He explicitly reaffirms the rule against ascribing spatiotemporal activity to God. When he details how divine and human activity interrelate in Christ, Schleiermacher insists that even in Christ's case, "God would have to remain strictly identical beyond all the means and measures of time."[21] The birth of Christ is the spatial-temporal effect of an eternal divine decree. It is the "appearance" of that eternal decree, "actualized in *one* point of space as well as in *one* period of time."[22] When Schleiermacher describes Christ's redemptive activity in greater detail, he explains that "the being of God in Christ is timeless and eternal even as an active principle."[23]

In his remarks about divine wisdom and love, in light of the feeling of redemption traced to Jesus, Schleiermacher follows a similar pattern: he describes divine activity in language that superficially, at least, implies temporality and spatiality; and then he qualifies that language by reiterating his canon that divine activity does not occur in time or space. Thus, for example, he defines love in general as "the orientation of wanting to unite with others and wanting to be in the other."[24] He goes on to make statements about divine love that sound similar to that general definition—for example, "the essence of divine love consists" in the "Supreme Being['s] communicat[ing] itself."[25] But Schleiermacher also reminds his readers that divine causality does not occur in time or space: for example, God's intelligence does not have time-bound features, and there is "no division or contrast in the divine causality anywhere."[26] We should conclude—I aver—that even here, at the end of his system of doctrine, Schleiermacher upholds his premise that divine activity does not occur in time or space.

As he did in his doctrine of creation, so also here, in his Christology and treatment of the divine attributes of wisdom and love, Schleiermacher seems willing to accept the opportunity cost of holding firm to the premise that divine activity does not occur in time or space. Christians frequently express the convictions that divine love heals what seems to us past healing, that divine love vivifies what lives no longer, and that God responds to our earnest petitions for wisdom by guiding us along our way. Schleiermacher's canon disallows—at least in dogmatic theology—anthropopathic interpretations of this divine wisdom and love.

He would expect us to apply the canon about divine activity to all such interpretations.

For example, Schleiermacher warns his readers to avoid interpreting events in a way that implies that individual persons as such are objects of divine love:

> If we want to view the life of individuals as the object of divine love, nevertheless, we cannot infer the divine love from advancements of life that are made at the expense of others, not if we do not want to sink back into the most grievous particularism, because then every time love would have appeared, its opposite would have done so as well.[27]

Schleiermacher explains that many of the events that individuals celebrate as evidence of God's specific love for them, as individuals, in fact depend on relative losses to other individuals: "in a great many respects promotion of one life is conditioned by negligence of others' lives."[28] The implied reason for this trade-off can be traced to the claim that finite things are completely causally interconnected. On Schleiermacher's premises, to identify isolated instances of God's love in the natural nexus is to subject divine activity to the contrasts that pervade the system of finite existence. Schleiermacher identifies divine love not at the level of the individual, in and for itself, but at the level of the human species. We see that divine activity is "protective and caring" insofar as we understand it to protect and care for the God-consciousness in human nature as such.[29]

Similarly, Schleiermacher warns his readers to avoid interpreting events in a way that implies that individual persons as such are objects of divine wisdom. He defines wisdom in general as "the proper outlining of designs, these designs being conceived in their manifold determinability and in the totality of their relationships to each other."[30] God's wise ordering of the world is a design that certainly includes all individuals. However, God does not have plans for individuals in and of themselves, but only for the whole of the world. Divine care is "actually directed" not to individuals as such, but only to their action,[31] and then only to their action in relation to the *one* aim of divine causality—namely, the "extension" and "development" of the church.[32] Schleiermacher concedes that we cannot discuss divine causality through divine attributes "without anthropomorphizing" and that our distinguishing between divine wisdom and divine love in the first place illustrates that anthropomorphizing, but he insists that the divine activity that we call "wisdom" and "love" does not occur in time or space.

I have argued that Schleiermacher applies his canon about divine activity rigorously and consistently. In his propositions about the world's beginning, and in those about the person of Christ, and in those about divine wisdom and love, Schleiermacher maintains that divine activity does not occur in time or space. I have also identified some of the significant opportunity costs that Schleiermacher was willing to absorb in his treatment of those major theological topics. But his position on divine activity also presents two significant advantages to ecotheologians.

The first advantage presented to ecotheologians by Schleiermacher's work on divine activity is that it underscores the urgent need for human beings to act. If the challenges of changes to planetary conditions—such as climate change, overpopulation, and mass extinctions—are indeed temporal-spatial, and divine activity does not occur in time or space, that seems to leave it to finite creatures to make the changes. Schleiermacher's view about divine activity incentivizes human action differently than most ecotheologians do. If we really believe that only finite activity will address global issues in space and time, then we could be more motivated to address them. Such an approach could be further developed by ecotheologians as a complement to theologies that use extended root metaphors for God's activity in which God is described as a closer analogue to human figures.

A second advantage of Schleiermacher's approach to divine activity is closely related to the first. If we are persuaded that God will not act in time or space to alter the course of events on planet Earth, we will have more motivation to understand the world in which we live, and to understand ourselves as a part of it, in order to act as wisely and effectively as we can. Schleiermacher did exactly that: he worked hard to gain a basic understanding of what scientists in his day were saying about the world and of the language and concepts they used to say it. The model that he builds in his theological description of the world shows how coherent and innovative a system of theology can be when the theologian who writes it deliberately expresses his theological claims within natural scientific frames. In the next section of this chapter, I will describe Schleiermacher's basic views about the world.

THE WORLD AS A DETERMINIST SYSTEM OF LIVING FORCES

Schleiermacher crafted his theological naturalism by integrating his views about divine activity with his views about creation. He wanted them to cohere perfectly with one another. I turn now to examine Schleiermacher's basic description of the world's structure and dynamism. While there are a few excellent studies of Schleiermacher's understanding of nature,[33] this aspect of his work has, in my opinion, yet to receive the comprehensive analysis that it deserves. Since little of the extant scholarship is written in

English,[34] I will provide readers with my own précis of Schleiermacher's view that the world is a system of living forces. Then I will give my reasons for believing that contemporary ecotheologians who engage closely and critically with Schleiermacher's description of the world could find it a widely helpful resource for their own proposals.

Ecotheologians make explicit and implicit claims about the structure, inventory, and causal activity of the world. Otherwise, they cannot hope to change the world. I think that Schleiermacher's general descriptions of the world's structure, inventory, and causal activity depend on three underlying, fundamental premises: first, every finite existent is an interplay of living "forces" (*Kräfte*), and all interactions between existents are interactions between living "forces"; second, the world as a whole is a living organism; and third, individual humans and social groups are organisms within this larger world-organism.

The first premise, that every finite thing is an interplay of forces, appears in Schleiermacher's work as early as his 1799 book, *On Religion: Speeches to Its Cultured Despisers,* and remains prominent through the rest of his career in teaching and writing. Schleiermacher took it as common knowledge that "each definite being" is composed of "two opposing forces" (*Kräften*)—"appropriation and repulsion" or "attraction and expansion."[35] This was Kant's well-known two-force explanation for material things.[36] Schleiermacher was correct to assume that his readers would be neither surprised nor alarmed by his claim that "this whole corporeal world . . . appears as . . . an eternally prolonged play of opposing forces."[37] In his 1814–15 lectures on *Dialektik,* Schleiermacher reiterates that "matter should be explained from a duplicity of forces."[38]

Schleiermacher soon adopted the view that every force is a "living" force. In those same 1814–15 lectures, he insisted that "everywhere that there is still formed matter, there is also still a substantial living force— even in the inorganic region."[39] In his lectures on psychology, he claimed that unformed matter, or matter as such, is only an abstraction or a general presupposition.[40] He denied that humans encounter matter that is formless and indeterminate and devoid of living force. Even the inorganic "somehow belongs to the realm of life and must participate in the general life."[41] At the most fundamental level, all interaction between things is an interaction of living force.

By choosing to explicate the dependence of finite things on God and the interactions between finite existents in causal terms, Schleiermacher moved the topic of causality to the center of his dogmatic theology—a distinctive mark of his work.[42] Three salient features of his causal explanations should be noted here. First, he very seldom distinguishes (in his oeuvre as a whole) between types of causes—for example, efficient, formal, material, and final—when he offers causal explanations for specific events. Second, Schleiermacher asserts that all finite causality is the causality of organisms: organisms are the only "true" causes.[43] Schleiermacher's natural nexus (*Naturzusammenhang*) is a story first and foremost about organisms.[44] Inorganic entities are merely "points of transition" for the causal activity that comes from living things. Third, in his system of doctrine Schleiermacher advocates a form of causal determinism. I think the gist of this determinism is sufficiently clear from three of his explicit claims. The first claim is that no event could have occurred otherwise than it did;[45] the second, that what determines any given event lies wholly within space and time;[46] and the third, that every event is determined not by one cause among several, but by finite reality as a whole.[47] I take these three claims to establish general, nonnegotiable boundaries for Schleiermacher's causal explanations.

The second premise—that the world is a living organism—is just as crucial as the first for interpreting Schleiermacher's theology. Schleiermacher eschewed Kant's careful adherence to the difference between investigating the world *as if* it were an organism (a regulative principle) and believing that the world *is* an organism (a constitutive principle).[48] Schleiermacher denied the basic conceptual distinction on which Kant had relied to mark the dividing line between the two modes of inquiry: "Contrary to Kant, constitutive and regulative principles do not admit of distinction."[49] In his own lectures on philosophical ethics, Schleiermacher asserted that the world *is* an organism: "the complete unity of finite being as the interrelation of nature and reason within an all-encompassing organism is the world."[50] In his system of doctrine, he abbreviates all of this with the term "natural nexus" (*Naturzusammenhang*).

One key corollary to Schleiermacher's view that the world is a living organism is that higher levels of existence explain lower levels—and not the other way around. Organic entities cannot be explained by inorganic elements. Schleiermacher viewed the latter as "mechanical," and insufficient explainers for the fact that "something continues to exist in its own right." Inorganic (mechanical) entities do not have the metaphysical wherewithal for relatively independent existence; that, says Schleiermacher, is "the sphere of the organic."[51] The world's being a living organism accounts for the organization of lower-level elements by higher ones.

Schleiermacher posits a hierarchy of existents that goes from lower, inchoate levels to higher, highly organized ones. At bottom are the inorganic entities composed of "elementary forces." The first recognizable form is crystallization, which does not yield "an enclosed whole" and thus has no enduring unity.[52] Organic entities, which do exhibit enduring unity, are divided into the vegetative, animal, and intelligent. Each of these levels has its own governing principle: "specific vivification" (*Belebung*) for vegetative life and "specific ensoulment" (*Beseelung*) for animal life.[53]

Human being is distinguished from other entities by its intelligence, which is its unique principle of organization (*Begeistung*).[54] Within the human organism, inorganic and vegetative and animal forces are not annihilated but harnessed or directed to higher ends. The perfection of human being can therefore be expressed as the perfect subordination of one's living forces to the intelligence.[55] That is what Schleiermacher means when—in his lectures on Christian ethics—he says that "the true goal" of religious ethics is "the complete dominion of spirit over flesh."[56]

According to Schleiermacher, the incarnation does not repair something previously finished but subsequently damaged (viz., human nature); rather, God's becoming human completes the creation of human nature.[57] The power of God-consciousness was in the original concept of human being and was present in a weak form at the beginning of the life of the species. That original power reached its perfection for the first time in the appearance of the Redeemer in history. In that sense, says Schleiermacher, the incarnation was the completion of the creation of human nature.

There is obviously a sense in which Schleiermacher believes that the earth belongs to humanity. Schleiermacher takes human being to be the turning point of earth's history, the highest organization that nature brings to life. He claims that the world was created for human being, in the person of the Redeemer. The planet has not been continuing a course of its own as God planned a recovery operation for humankind. Rather, the world has one story only: all of history has been a suspenseful preparation for "the revelation of God in the flesh."[58]

Yet in other respects, Schleiermacher subordinates the human species to its planetary and cosmic contexts. "We live in and from nature and for it," he writes.[59] He describes humanity as "a depiction of a single modification of [the universe's] elements."[60] Many products of the earth exist; human being is merely one of them. Schleiermacher constantly emphasizes the radical nature of our interconnections to all other finite things. He does this by stressing the web of finite relations in which humans are embedded. This is what he seems to indicate, for example, by the remark that humankind is "only a product of the Earth and the Earth itself a product of the cosmic system."[61]

The third general premise that underlies Schleiermacher's description of the world is that individual humans and social groups are organisms within the larger world-organism. Human individuals and their social groups are not somewhat like baseline biological units at a much smaller scale; rather, both individuals and groups *actually are* organisms. Schleiermacher treats not only individuals but also families,[62] peoples, states,[63] religions,[64] and the human species[65] as natural wholes that stand in nested, organic relations to one another. The church,[66] the main unit of Christian ethics, is no different in this respect: "Like every other ordered human association, the Christian church is an organic whole."[67]

Schleiermacher's description of the world—much like his account of divine activity—could be a widely helpful resource for contemporary eco-theologians who engage with this part of his work closely and critically. First, Schleiermacher demonstrates that he can use his description of the world to craft creative alternative explanations of several traditional doctrines. For example, Schleiermacher tells the entire story of redemption in organicist terms. In the second part of his system, when he offers his most detailed description of the interrelation of divine and human in Christ, he rejects the standard two-nature account[68] in favor of an analogy derived from, and internal to, his understanding of what an organism is:

> The being of God in the Redeemer is posited as his innermost primary force [*Grundkraft*], from which all his activity proceeds and which holds all the elements of his life together. However, everything human simply forms the organism for this primary force and relates itself to the same as its system both for taking this [primary force] in and for and presenting it, just as in us all other forces have to relate to our intelligence.[69]

Christology is not the only part of traditional doctrine that Schleiermacher reconceives through his description of the world as a system of living forces. He reiterates his organism analogy in each of the remaining major topics in the system of doctrine. The relation of the Intelligence to all other powers in the organism (that is human being) is the basis for understanding not only the relation of the divine to all that is human in Christ, but also the relation of Christ to the church (ecclesiology), to individual believers, to the rest of humanity (theological anthropology), and to Christian Scriptures.[70] Schleiermacher delivers a single, coherent, organicist story.

Schleiermacher enhanced the coherence of his system of doctrine by describing the incarnation of God in human consciousness as one more instance of a general structural feature of organic life. Just as each major class of organisms has a "principle of organization" that arranges the forces at play in its member entities, so, too, Christ's absolutely powerful God-consciousness has become the new principle of organization for human nature.[71] Prior to Jesus, our species "had existed only in a provisional state,"[72] because human God-consciousness was at provisional strength. When individuals become believers, even the way that they structure and process sensory inputs changes.[73] Hierarchically arranged principles of organization—in plants, animals, Christ, and the church—form one and the same natural nexus.[74]

Third, key elements in Schleiermacher's description of the world already resonate beautifully with some contemporary ecotheologies, and readers could explore those elements in greater detail and then critically develop them in creative proposals of their own. For example, Schleiermacher's description of the natural nexus, the *Naturzusammenhang,* as a web of causal interaction is as rigorous and distinctive today as it was the day that he wrote it, and could make a fine complement to ecotheologies that emphasize nature "as an interrelated system."[75] Schleiermacher's view that all matter is living force and that social groups are organisms within a larger world-organism resonates with elements of Gaian ecotheology and Gaian theory.[76] It might also prove advantageous to ecotheologians who work with new materialist ontologies and descriptions of agency. These contemporary forms of materialism assume what political theorist Jane Bennett calls "vibrant matter."[77]

ADVANTAGES OF SCHLEIERMACHER'S THEOLOGICAL NATURALISM

Few ecotheological readers will agree with all of Schleiermacher's views about creation (i.e., his views about the relationship between God and the world, and about the world's origin, structure, and dynamism). But Schleiermacher presents a distinctive theological naturalism that offers significant potential value to contemporary ecotheologians. I have discussed two features of his views that I think are especially rich and provocative: first, when Schleiermacher reflects on what his religious experiences imply about God, he comes to the conclusion that God does not act in time or space; second, and relatedly, when he reflects on what his religious experiences imply about the world, he comes to the conclusion that it is a determinist system of living forces.

I will close with brief observations about what it could mean, specifically, to continue thinking with Schleiermacher about sustainability issues. What tasks could be next for those who would like to build Schleiermacher-inspired ecotheologies? I have two points to suggest. First, in order to produce viable proposals about sustainability that draw from Schleiermacher's work, ecotheologians will need both to focus on a specific question in sustainability conversations and to read widely in his work. Schleiermacher could offer help in all three of the major components in discussions about sustainability—environment, economy, and equity. For example, Schleiermacher's description of the world as a system of living forces provides a model for using a central feature of the world—in his case, configurations of living force—to organize discussion on multiple issues. Schleiermacher's ethics, which continue his organicist commitments, could contribute to new proposals in planetary ethics—which would apply to questions about the environment, economy, and equity (or justice). All along, Schleiermacher's insistence that divine activity does not occur in time or space would foreground the urgency and responsibility of human action toward sustainable living.

Second, and related to the first, an excellent way to continue thinking critically and creatively with Schleiermacher about ecology and sustainability is to ask, if divine activity does not occur in time or space, then when or where does it occur? While Schleiermacher chose to forgo a raft of popular and comforting stories that Christians tell about who God is and how, when, and where God acts in the world; about how the world's energies are organized and how they move; and about how humans ought to understand themselves as part of this world, he obviously did claim that divine activity is (in some way) real and that Christians must not reduce it to the activity of finite things. Ecotheologians who modify Schleiermacher's theological naturalism for use in proposals about sustainability have an exciting opportunity to explore how Christians may describe nontemporal, nonspatial divine activity in our present context.

To express their Christian experience of divine activity conceptually, and then to articulate what that experience implies about planetary conditions and about the place of humans within Earth's system, ecotheologians may need to reconceive traditional Christian doctrines. Schleiermacher did not anticipate that human activity could trigger catastrophic, global changes in Earth's system. But he did provide an excellent model for ecotheologians who are willing to reexamine Christian experience and then to articulate it conceptually in ways that cohere with the best of what we think we know about the present world.

CONCLUSION

Schleiermacher's theological naturalism is a bold attempt to describe Christian religious experiences as natural experiences. His interpretation of the relationship between finite existence and its source (viz., God) depends on two crucial theses. The first is that divine activity does not occur in time or space. Hence God is essentially noninterventionist in time and space. The second is that nature is a nexus of radically interconnected, living forces, in which every event (including human being) is wholly determined by what precedes it in time and space. Schleiermacher's provocative conclusions from these two claims actually present contemporary ecotheologians with promising critical resources with which to craft new proposals for ecologically sustainable living.

4

DIVINE PROVIDENCE AND HUMAN FREEDOM IN THE QUEST FOR ECOLOGICAL LIVING

Anette I. Hagan

"Providence" is the traditional theological term for God's activity in the world. The Latin root of the term, *providentia*, means foresight or foreknowledge and implies that the world is under God's beneficent care and guidance. David Fergusson defines providence as "the infinite resourcefulness of God in dealing with human creatures in a manner that is in accordance with the purposes disclosed and fulfilled in Christ."[1] While a modern secular conception of the world considers nature and history as relatively self-contained systems of interrelated factors that are subject to natural explanation, for Christian theology the concept of divine agency is necessary. On many accounts, these two seem incompatible:[2] either processes in nature and history occur entirely unconditionally and are independent of any divine or transcendent power, or a divine agency is assumed to operate, and this is then credited with providentially shaping the course of nature and history. Friedrich Schleiermacher's understanding of providence overcomes this impasse. He posits a dynamic relation between divine providence and the interconnected process of nature and history by interpreting divine agency in a way that allows for free, contingent actions and events within the world. At the same time, he upholds the teleological nature of divine agency, whose ultimate goal for the human race is the redemptive reign of God. It is implicit in this view that human action, despite digressions, wrong turns, errors, and mistakes, remains on the trajectory toward the reign of God, in which everyone will ultimately be redeemed.

As we have seen in chapter 2, crucial to Schleiermacher's interpretation of providence is the concept of one single eternal divine decree to create, sustain, and redeem the natural world, that is, the interconnected process of nature that constitutes this planet. Applied exclusively to the human aspect of the universe, this means that everything is created and preserved for the supreme purpose of the redemption of the human race in Christ. Every individual will be redeemed as part of the world through God's providential resourcefulness: "the ordering within which redemption is realized in each person is the same thing as the carrying out of the divine ordering of the world in relation to that person."[3] Schleiermacher's understanding of the doctrine of providence thus has implications for his view of the world and the human race as it is determined by the divine decree and at the same time contingent with regard to individual actions and events. Schleiermacher tried to "avoid both mechanistic deism and pantheism"[4] in his attempt to delineate providence.

In *Christian Faith*, he does not expound a fully fledged doctrine of providence, nor does he actually employ the term "providence," *Vorsehung*, more than twice.[5] The expression, he argues, is of an alien origin. It has been transferred from non-Christian writers to teachers in the Christian church, and this crossover has impeded a clear presentation of distinctively Christian faith. This situation, he continues, could have been avoided if the scriptural terms "predetermination" (*Vorherbestimmung*) and "foreordination" (*Vorherversehung*)[6] had been used instead of "providence." Schleiermacher further rejects the term because it belies a particular one-sidedness in that it refers to the "determination of a particular without consideration of what would naturally ensue from its coexistence with everything else."[7] Schleiermacher's view of the world and its constituents or existents is always from the perspective of the whole rather than individual beings, actions, or events. He therefore consistently employs the term "preservation" (*Erhaltung*) for those aspects of the wider doctrine of creation that are discussed in the context of what dogmatic tradition refers to as "providence." Although *Christian Faith* contains a separate discussion of the doctrine of preservation,[8] the concept of divine providence with all its implications is so central to the Christian pious self-consciousness that it pervades the whole work. Moreover, it is made explicit in relation to a number of different doctrines. Taken together, the doctrine of preservation and the other relevant but dispersed statements in *Christian Faith* offer a coherent doctrine of providence.

This chapter extends the focus of the previous chapter on creation by exploring the theological implications of *Christian Faith* that are relevant to the interconnectedness of nature and the history of human beings, and the wider concept of providence: divine causality, absolute dependence on God, preservation, original perfection of the world, and soteriology. Possible consequences for ecological living will be discussed throughout each of these sections. Even though such consequences cannot be directly derived from Schleiermacher's concepts of divine causality and finite agency, they do adhere to it. His understanding of God's providential agency entails that the redeemed act freely in accordance with the divine decree to create, sustain, and redeem the interconnected process of nature. Human beings who have been redeemed are motivated to live in ecologically sustainable ways and—by living in communities of partly redeemed and partly yet unredeemed persons—to encourage others to do likewise.

Therefore, far from leading to human complacency, inactivity, or indeed despondency based on the belief that the ultimate fate of the world has already been decreed, the divine decree and its implementation in human beings and the natural order actually ensure that the contingent actions of these free agents are directed toward the ultimate consummation of the reign of God by sustaining the planet for future generations, yet to be redeemed.

DIVINE CAUSALITY

For Schleiermacher, the existence and shape of the causal nexus of the created world in which humanity finds itself and which stimulates stirrings of pious self-consciousness are entirely due to divine causality. In this sense, divine activity is in accordance with the law-governed course of nature. However, no demands can be made on divine causality that extend beyond the natural order.[9] As a consequence, no relevant dogmatic statements can be posited about what God might be or have been outside and before the creation of the world. From the perspective of the pious self-consciousness of human beings, divine and finite causality are therefore coextensive: they are equal in their scope. This observation, however, does not imply that divine and finite causality are identical or that the interconnected process of nature is determined in each particular aspect by God's agency. Divine agency is different in kind from the processes of nature and history. It is also different from particular causes set in motion by finite beings.

Finite causality is temporal, local, and multifarious, whereas divine causality is eternal, omnipresent, and simple.[10] Finite beings are endowed with particular and partial causality, whereas divine causality is universal and absolute or unconditional. All finite activity is measurable in time and space, but divine causality is absolutely nontemporal and nonspatial.[11] Moreover, Schleiermacher writes, "Everything that happens temporally and spatially also has its conditions in the totality of what is outside it and before it, however much these factors might be hidden from us thus far, and to that extent everything that happens falls under the category of a specially ordered use of power."[12] Actions and events take place under influences beyond themselves; they become what they are only because of their particular temporal and spatial place within the interconnected process of nature. Contingent actions at the moment of activity co-form this process.

Christian Faith has no separate doctrine of God, but Schleiermacher discusses divine attributes in each material part.[13] Part 1 (§§32–61), which is concerned with religious self-consciousness as such, explicates divine attributes in an innovative way. The traditional dogmatic concept of eternity is here identified with God's absolutely timeless causality as opposed to finite causality in time. It conditions everything temporal as well as time itself, and it conditions everything spatial and space itself. The traditional divine attribute of omnipotence is identified with God's causality. More precisely, omnipotence is expressed as divine causality when viewed as encompassing the totality of natural causality.[14] Each particular act and event in the interconnected process of nature is both causative and caused. As a consequence, divine omnipotence cannot simply supplement natural causes. That means that God does not intervene in the process of nature, as Edward Waggoner has demonstrated in the previous chapter. Schleiermacher rejects the notion of supernatural miracles. In fact, there is no causal relation at all between God and any particular effect in the world, singled out from others. God is equally immediate to all events and activities within the process of nature. For God there is no distinction between the general and the particular, nor between the actual and the possible. The totality of God's causality is entirely different from that which belongs to the sphere of reciprocal action within the world, but divine agency is a necessary precondition of all activity. Human agency cannot constitute itself and cannot be completely explained as the result of other finite agencies.[15]

Schleiermacher's providential understanding of divine causality and his teleological understanding of history can easily lead to a determinist concept of history; according to this view, history unfolds exactly in accordance with the exhaustive divine decree. Michael Root's criticism of Schleiermacher's system is a case in point: Root concludes that in Schleiermacher's system "history in its final entirety is the only possible history."[16] Similarly, Edwin van Driel notes that since there is no gap between divine ability and divine willing, and between possibility and reality, divine causality exhausts all possibilities, and there is no alternative for reality as it is.[17] However, Root's and van Driel's observations disregard the fact that in Schleiermacher's concept, God does not determine individual historical or natural events or individual acts as single events or single acts: "Within the totality of finite being only a particular and partial causality befits each individual item . . . ; general causality exists only in that source whereupon the totality of this divided causality is itself dependent."[18] Schleiermacher's contention that for God possibility and reality coincide does not mean that everything is absolutely, rather than relatively, determined. Rather, as Schleiermacher explains, "Everything is and comes to be entirely through the interconnected process of nature, with the result that each part persists by means of all and everything persists entirely by divine omnipotence."[19] In other words, every event and action that occur through finite causality are posited as occurring by divine omnipotence already. God determines the whole absolutely and the particulars in relation to that whole.

Colin Gunton observes that a weakness of determinist-seeming theology is that "eschatology is so determined by protology that the end is effectively determined by the beginning, and history is apparently closed to the re-creating work of the Spirit."[20] Such a theology is indifferent to responsible moral action, including, of course, ecologically responsible living. Gunton's observation regarding determinist theology, however, cannot be applied to Schleiermacher's conception for two reasons. First, the single eternal divine decree that Schleiermacher posits encompasses both creation and ultimate redemption. Beginning and end thus do not determine each other; they are both subsumed under the one universal decree that determines everything. Second, in Schleiermacher's understanding of providence, the *telos* of God's creation and human history, namely the eschatological redemption of the human race and the natural world, is predetermined, but individual historical events are not. The Holy Spirit is at work throughout history.

B. L. Hebblethwaite comments that in "a deterministic universe the future is present in its causes."[21] His observation can be applied to Schleiermacher's conception only to a limited degree, either with the qualification that no single cause determines a future single act or event or with the qualification that the totality of all finite causes will ultimately issue in the redemption of the whole human race. The intent of God's agency is indeed soteriological.[22] As Richard R. Niebuhr states, for Schleiermacher, Christian faith is confident that "history and the self belong to the good . . . of the divine good-pleasure."[23] God's "good-pleasure" is a way of characterizing God's love for the world God has created and preserves, but, with Niebuhr, "it is not the judgment of history on what history has produced."[24] In other words, not everything that happens in the world or everything that history has produced is good simply because of God's good pleasure in creation. Eschatologically, however, everything will be subsumed under God's grace.

Unless Schleiermacher's concept of the teleological unfolding of nature and history through contingent actions and events is clearly explicated, there is a danger in applying the doctrine of preservation to issues of ecological living. That doctrine could then lead Christians to resign themselves to passive trust in the divinely determined course of nature and history. Schleiermacher's concept, however, does not elicit resignation as an appropriate response to a predetermined outcome, since the divine plan enables and sustains contingent secondary causes. Hence, it does not allow persons of faith to simply sit back and do nothing in the certainty that everything will be set right in the goodness of time. More broadly, Schleiermacher's understanding of Christianity as a teleological religion actually calls forth activity. Human beings not only have free will and find themselves faced with real choice of actions, they must exercise their freedom of choice and act in one way or another.

What does this mean for ecological living? Although Schleiermacher had no concept at all of the means and processes human beings have developed to potentially make Earth uninhabitable, we can extrapolate from his doctrine of preservation that the redeemed ought to act in ways that help sustain the planet and avert climate catastrophes, for instance by using renewable energy sources and reducing their carbon footprint. Today this living world subsists by way of distinct ecological systems that sustain life and that encompass Earth itself. Divine creation and preservation, according to Schleiermacher, ensure that the freedom and the power to act, which are given to all finite agents to exercise this agency within the divinely ordained, interconnected processes of nature and history, are continually sustained. Secondary causes themselves are also objects of divine preservation, and the same applies to the very range of causes that exist within the process of nature: even the freest cause is ordained by God. Nevertheless, Schleiermacher's concept allows for the caveat that as God enables the agency of human beings, some of these agents, as J. R. Lucas writes, "may refuse to play."[25] As relatively autonomous agents they may choose any course of action, including activities that do not further or indeed counteract sustainability. But any such setbacks are temporary and will eventually be overcome by other contingent actions, so that ultimately the reign of God can be expected to be consummated. In the context of the divine government of the world, Schleiermacher explicitly states that we are "not to view the natural world in such a way that it goes its own way by virtue of divine preservation and that the divine government of the world exercises influence on it only through special particular acts designed to bring it into conformity with the reign of grace."[26] Rather, divine government and preservation are two sides of the same coin.

Clearly, such concerns and positive measures taken to sustain life and natural resources are not a prerogative or responsibility pertaining to Christians alone. Relatively free agency, world-immanent causality, and spontaneity are upheld in Schleiermacher's concept for all finite beings. Contingent actions shape the planet on which humans find themselves. The actions of the redeemed ought to be ecologically responsible because this is a precondition for keeping the planet fit for future generations and for furthering the divine decree toward the reign of God. At the same time, trust in God's decree to sustain the cosmos in existence by grounding all events in the interconnected process of nature—despite human actions that actively work against this sustaining decree by driving climate change and by exploiting fossil fuels for personal or corporate gain—is an incentive for Christians to work to reverse this trend. The changelessness of the divine decree induces confidence in God and the achievement of God's ultimate purpose. It does not, however, excuse anyone from their current responsibility to act toward reversing this trend.

ABSOLUTE DEPENDENCE UPON GOD
AND HUMANITY'S RELATIVE FREEDOM

In Schleiermacher's *Christian Faith*, God remains an entirely formal concept until the discussion of the relationship between God and the world in §§50–56. However, right from the start of the material part 1 (§§32–61), the inalienable relation of God to Christ is made explicit. Schleiermacher maintains that in Christian pious self-consciousness "there could be no relation to Christ that would not be a relation to God as well," and vice versa.[27] Part 1 of *Christian Faith* deals with religious or pious self-consciousness "as it is always already presupposed by, but also always contained in, every Christian religious stirring of mind and heart."[28] Part 2 (§§62–169) is concerned first with Christian self-consciousness as it is determined by sin, and second as it is determined by grace. To the extent that Christian self-consciousness cannot really be conceived properly without reference to sin and grace, this division is of course abstract. So, despite the formal design or layout, the doctrines explicated in part 2 apply to part 1, too: the christological trajectory toward redemption has to be taken into account from the very beginning, even though the actual doctrine of Christ is only expounded in the second section of part 2. Christology, or the doctrine of Christ the Redeemer, is intrinsic to Schleiermacher's whole system of doctrine, in which, as Robert Sherman writes, all parts "cohere in virtually seamless interrelation."[29]

What does Schleiermacher mean by the term "God"? In his introduction to *Christian Faith*, he identifies "God" purely formally with the "whence" of our feeling of absolute dependence, or the source of our receptive and self-initiated active existence.[30] The feeling of absolute dependence is one and the same thing as the consciousness of oneself as in relation with God. Hence, Schleiermacher argues, "absolute dependence is the fundamental relation that all other relations must include within themselves."[31] In Matthias Gockel's words, absolute dependence is a characteristic "of the ontological structure of humanity,"[32] whether individual human beings ever become conscious of it or not. Absolute dependence also implies an asymmetrical relationship in which there is no reciprocity between human and divine actions. God is absolutely independent, which means that, as Bruce Boyer explains, "nothing at all causally affects God."[33] God does not temporally react to whatever unfolds in the world.

The feeling of absolute dependence reflects the fact that human beings are conscious of themselves as being part of creation or, more precisely, of being placed within the general interconnected process of nature.[34] Since human beings exist in the world alongside each other and alongside other finite agents whom they influence and by whom they, in turn, are influenced, absolute freedom does not exist within the created world. But there is always a degree of reciprocity between different finite agents, who are both active and receptive to each other. In this sense, finite beings exercise relative freedom and experience relative dependence with regard to other agents and events in the world. Finite beings choose and act freely within the parameters they find already given by God's agency. The divine decree offers possibilities for them to choose from, and they realize different options and reject others through the use of their relative freedom.[35] In this sense, it is necessary that they act freely and contingently and not under coercion by a divine will that overrules human choices. Therefore, for human beings to act at all is to act freely and contingently. By divine ordination, freedom within the world is a mandatory attribute of being human. As Eilert Herms puts it, "Schleiermacher, with unequalled consequence, represents the transcendental sense of the Christian doctrine of creation [and preservation] as a theory about the conditions for the possibility of the lot of finite freedom."[36]

However, because the world is absolutely dependent on God and God has decreed to sustain it, according to Schleiermacher's conception, human agents cannot destroy it. He does not explicitly deny this possibility, but his claims about absolute dependence necessarily imply such a reading. Absolute dependence entails that the ultimate fate of the planet lies in God's hands. However, human beings exercise their freedom to act within the world to either further God's decree or (from the human perspective) to work against it. In doing so, human beings not only have relative freedom but also are relatively dependent on other free agents and causes, such as natural occurrences. Human actions cause reactions and invariably have consequences. These will take either negative forms, such as environmental changes like deforestation leading to drought or flooding, or positive forms like environmental living and ecologically sustaining actions to preserve the planet. Both are grounded in the relative freedom of human beings within the interdependent process of nature.

THE DOCTRINE OF PRESERVATION

Schleiermacher describes Christian religious self-consciousness vis-à-vis the God-world relation in the doctrine of creation (§§36–49). In accordance with traditional doctrinal works, but only for the sake of clarity,

Schleiermacher divides this topos into two propositions: the world is created by God, and God preserves the world.[37] Creation and preservation are two inextricably linked aspects of the single divine decree. The creative act of God is not limited to the original event of the actual creation of the world but extends in time to the present and to the future consummation of the world in the reign of God. God's continuous creative activity corresponds to God's continuous activity in the reign of grace.[38] In *Christian Faith*, the doctrine of creation does not offer any statements about how the world began, nor does it describe the mechanics of its existence in time. Instead, it presents "a preliminary understanding of the world as the catalyst for the emergence and continuity of the fundamental feeling of absolute dependence as it is perceived by Christians."[39] The universal divine decree to create and redeem subsumes creation under preservation and orders creation in relation to redemption. Thus, by exploring the development of Christian religious self-consciousness from the point of view of human beings as they interpret the world as divine creation, Schleiermacher "employs Christ as the hermeneutical key for interpreting creation."[40] For this reason, many implications of creation have their goal in Christ the Redeemer. Indeed, as the previous chapter demonstrates, Schleiermacher posits redemption as the completion of creation.

The doctrine of creation proper, without regard to preservation, culminates in the statement that "our feeling of absolute dependence could not be referred to the general constitution of all finite being if anything within it were, or ever had been, independent of God."[41] The feeling of absolute dependence is simply a reflection of the fact that all creation depends absolutely on God. The doctrine of preservation proper in *Christian Faith* explicates the actual proposition (§46), the relation of the natural and the miraculous to the natural order (§47), the pleasant and the unpleasant (§48), and free and natural causes (§49). For the purpose of this chapter, §§46 and 49 are of particular importance.

As Martin Redeker summarizes in his introduction to the seventh German edition (1960) of *Christian Faith*, the world is synonymous with the totality of diversity, finiteness, and transitoriness, whereas God is the absolute unity. God is the ultimate causality and as such not only the creative source of everything there is but also the very precondition for the causal nexus of the world.[42] In Schleiermacher's words, "Religious self-consciousness—by virtue of which we locate all that bestirs us and influences us within our absolute dependence on God—wholly coincides with our discernment that precisely all of this is conditioned and determined by the interconnected process of nature."[43] The world is thus posited as a creation of absolute divine determination. Preservation encompasses the movements and changes that affect the created world and its existents as a whole but not with regard to individual existents and their internal being.

Absolute dependence of all that happens on God, and natural causation as the complete conditionality of all that happens, are two sides of the same coin. The emphasis here is on the term "totality": Schleiermacher is keen to avoid any atomistic interpretation of the system of nature according to which an individual action or event is caused by another single act or occurrence. Instead, Schleiermacher argues, every individual occurrence is dependent on the totality of all others in the interconnected process of nature[44] and must be seen as the product of the operation of chains of cause and effect. Only the sum total of all finite activity and passivity is identical in content with the system of nature.[45]

Since all events in the world have the potential to stimulate human pious self-consciousness, Schleiermacher maintains that natural causes and explanations can never be perceived as a threat to piety. Moreover, "all events in the natural order are appropriate objects of scientific research."[46] The advance of science and the increasing scientific explanations of hitherto unexplainable natural events do not entail a corresponding decrease in piety since natural occurrences are not directly caused by divine intervention in the first place. For Schleiermacher, the interests of science and religion are entirely compatible and can thrive simultaneously. For Christians pursuing research into environmental disasters and into ways of sustainable living, Schleiermacher's modern understanding is therefore positively empowering.

Since preservation subsumes everything there is, any differentiation of particular target audiences of divine preservation is superfluous. Accordingly, Schleiermacher rejects the traditional distinction between general, special, and most special providence, where the first applies to the world in general, the second to the human race, and the third to individuals. He similarly abolishes the distinction between preserving and cooperating divine activities. Since everything is uniformly and absolutely dependent on God, anything independent of God that could then cooperate with God would have to be posited outside the relation of absolute dependence. Thus, Schleiermacher maintains, "by means of all powers that are distributed and preserved in the world, everything happens or can happen as God originally and continually willed it."[47]

What does this mean for the state of our planet, which can be taken to be synonymous with Schleiermacher's "interconnected process of nature"? Is the present ecological condition of Earth the way it is because God decrees it to be that way? How can its precarious ecological state be reconciled with the aspect of the divine decree that relates to the preservation of creation? Schleiermacher would argue that the divine decree guarantees the *telos* of the planet and all finite being on it, and that neither natural nor historical catastrophes present a contradiction of the decree to sustain creation. This is the case because the decree applies to the world as a whole and not to individual events in themselves. All human actions and choices are contingent and voluntary, and the fact that finite beings must act freely within the interconnected process of nature is simply the corollary of the divine decree through which this process is set in motion and maintained. As Schleiermacher observes, "Within the totality of finite being only a particular and partial causality befits each individual item, in that each is dependent not on *one* other item but on *all other* items."[48] There is "no productive relation"[49] between God and a particular finite effect in the world, and the universal divine decree extends only to individual human beings insofar as they are part of the human race and the interconnected process of nature.

In this sense, the totality of all events and actions understood historically is identical with the one all-encompassing act of God.[50] In the finite causal nexus, all events and activities are results of and, in turn, impulses for other events and activities. Schleiermacher rejects any understanding in which God overrides or undercuts the system of causes and effects operational in the natural world. Rather, God subsumes them all under the divine decree.[51]

Living ecologically in ways that help sustain the planet for future generations means freely choosing to act in accordance with God's decree to preserve creation. However, human beings also have, and clearly use, the freedom not to act in such ways. Nevertheless, God's decree not only determines the direction of travel toward the reign of God, viewed as the ultimate goal of the human race, but God's agency also uses what is evil for what is good. Schleiermacher, who lived in largely preindustrial Prussia, could not observe any environmental evil on the scale reached over the past two centuries. But it would not constitute a violation of his system of doctrine to include humanly caused evil against organically structured, nonhuman ecological systems within the natural environment alongside evil that bears social and individual moral effects.[52] As the next chapter will show, the world in which humans live is inconceivable without evil. Yet evil does not exist in its own right. What is evil is defined in contrast to what is good, and in ordinary circumstances good is also qualified by the presence of evil. Thus, trusting in God's providence, we may hope that something that enters human life and adversely affects the ecological system as an evil will ultimately be turned into what is good within the interconnected process of nature. Natural evils not caused by humans can be borne as such, because they belong to the natural order created by God. Indeed, Dawn DeVries and Brian Gerrish warn that "to exempt evil from the divine causality would be to raise the specter of a cosmic dualism."[53]

Since the consciousness of free will is compatible with the feeling of absolute dependence,[54] Schleiermacher-inspired Christians may try to weave freely chosen ecological living into the fabric of a Christian way of life. According to Schleiermacher, the more predominant a person's God-consciousness, the greater that person's willingness to freely act in accordance with the divine decree to preserve creation. Only free actions of finite beings enable morality and responsibility. In the sense that human actions are not determined by material or social causes, they are relatively free or spontaneous. Where such secondary causes determine human actions, they are understood to be relatively dependent. But whether humans act spontaneously or in relative dependence on other factors, or if there is an admixture of both, in the interconnected process of nature, in Schleiermacher's understanding, human freedom is compatible with divine determination of the whole of creation. With the totality of all individual actions and events leading to the reign of God, humanity can take comfort in the understanding that no matter what contingent actions seem to derail this trajectory, God will ultimately sustain and preserve the system of nature until the consummation of the Christian church. In this way, as Robert Sherman observes, Schleiermacher's doctrine of preservation emphasizes the "development in history, the dynamism of nature, and through divine governance and human intervention, the gradual amelioration of the world's evils."[55] Certainly, human beings are intended for development, and Karl Barth even ventures the observation that for Schleiermacher, the reign of God is "utterly and unequivocally identical with the advance of civilization."[56] Whether or not such an optimistic view of progress as Schleiermacher's can still be adopted today is open to discussion. In his system, scientific investigations into nature and the interest of piety converge when full scientific knowledge of the world has been achieved. At that point it will be found to be identical with the full knowledge of the interconnected system of nature. That said, Schleiermacher himself was also one of the first theologians who foresaw the modern conflict between science and religion, where the advance of science and the retreat of religion are directly correlated. We cannot simply emulate now Schleiermacher's purported consonance of faith and modern sciences. Moreover, the optimistic scientific worldview of German idealist philosophy, according to which science and progress went hand in hand, has collapsed with the invention of modern systems of mass destruction.

Schleiermacher lived at a time when the very idea that the planet could be destroyed by human action was utterly inconceivable. But this is now a very real possibility with regard to environmental issues such as the destruction of species (including humans), scarcity of clean water, unprecedented climate change, and exhaustion of traditional natural resources. Of course, the situation is even more drastically different now in view of the nuclear forces that can be unleashed at the press of a button. However, without perhaps sharing Schleiermacher's overly optimistic outlook, we can share his contention that, despite appearances, humanity is on the trajectory toward the reign of God. Trust in God's governance and God's decree for the preservation of the created world goes hand in hand with hope for human progress. An increasing awareness of the precarious state of the planet and the willingness and ability to work toward sustaining it are certainly compatible with Schleiermacher's understanding of preservation.

Christian Faith §49 states that both the mechanism of nature and the activity of finite causes are ordered by God. God's creative activity and God's activity governing creation are the precondition for everything that happens in the world and stem from a single, uninterrupted divine act. From the human perspective, the activity of divine agents unfolds, for the most part, progressively and bit by bit over the course of history. Robert Sherman aptly suggests in this context that Schleiermacher's conception of divine and human causality replaces the traditional linear model— according to which events in the world are either traced back to God as the first mover or up to God as the providential governor—with a concentric model.[57] Schleiermacher conceptualizes causality as two concentric circles. The inner circle represents finite causality with real, given, spontaneous freedom of finite agents, while the outer circle, which represents divine causality, encompasses, limits, and sustains the inner circle. God empowers and preserves finite causality as an integrated process without intervening at any point in time or space. By upholding each finite existent in its being, God upholds free agents and causes as such.

THE ORIGINAL PERFECTION OF THE WORLD

For Schleiermacher, the terms "creation" and "preservation" signify not the beginning and the continuation of the world as two separate events but the created world as it is sustained by God. The constitution of this world and its original perfection are discussed in the third section of the doctrine of creation in *Christian Faith* (§§57–61). Assuming with traditional dogmatic accounts that in its original state both the world and the metaphorical first pair, Adam and Eve, were perfect, what has happened to humanity, and how did the world get into the desolate state in which it is now? Schleiermacher's interpretation employs an understanding of the concept of original perfection that is different from much that is represented in traditional doctrine. For Schleiermacher, the term does not designate some primordial state of the world before or outside the existence of human beings, nor some perfect ontological structure of the first pair. Moreover, he asserts that original perfection of the world and of human beings cannot be considered in isolation of each other: "there can be talk only of original perfection of the world in relation to humankind."[58]

Schleiermacher explains that original perfection of the world has two aspects: it relates to the "natural subsistence of human organization,"[59] which God has put in place to conduct all other finite being to what has spirit, and the "knowability" (*Erkennbarkeit*)[60] of the world overall. Both aspects ensure the continuity of religious self-consciousness within the totality of creation, with the result that the innate human capacity for an ultimately uninterrupted God-consciousness cannot be lost. The perfection of the world thus consists in two things: human beings are endowed with the ability to lead other finite beings in the world toward the reign of God, and human beings can know the world and its existents and distinguish these from human self-consciousness. Within the world, thus originally perfect, the necessary conditions are in place for human beings to know or recognize aspects of the world that affect their self-consciousness and stir the development of their God-consciousness. An increasing awareness of the world and creation goes hand in hand with a growing God-consciousness and, it can be argued, could motivate Christians to preserve the world since original perfection has never been lost.

Similarly, Schleiermacher does not understand original perfection of human beings as a onetime state of innocence or as the ability not to sin. Rather, the term signifies the human capacity to receive grace or, as Dawn DeVries puts it, "the possibility for the actualization of God-consciousness both within the human race as a whole and within humanity."[61] Longing for communion with God, even if a person is unconscious of such yearning, is an anthropological constant, an inalienable characteristic of being human. This longing belongs to the original perfection of human nature.[62] It cannot be annulled by sin. Hence no sin, including the first sin of the supposed first human pair, has the potential to destroy the world or to totally corrupt human nature. The original perfection of the world in relation to human beings has been present from the very beginning and has always remained the same, and it is guaranteed by the perfection and blessedness of Christ himself. Otherwise, Schleiermacher argues, "along with human nature the entire arrangement of the planet in relation to humankind would have been altered as well."[63]

There is a corollary of this optimism for ecological living: no matter how far human destruction of the planet, its climate zones, and its natural resources has gone and may still proceed, it is ultimately indestructible by human agents. Faith in God's decree is again reflected in the fabric of Christian life lived in an ecologically sustaining way. By virtue of having been redeemed, Christians receive the spiritual impulse to act in ways that can sustain the world both as individual agents and as a community.

SOTERIOLOGY

The redemptive work of Christ not only is intrinsic to the whole of *Christian Faith*, it also provides the trajectory as well as the goal of divine providence. Redemption is wrought through the communication of Christ's sinless perfection. His perfection, which occurs in the incarnation, cannot be explained from within the context of the interconnected process of nature. Although Christ appears in history, his appearance cannot be deduced from history.[64]

The purpose of Christ's mission is to restore "what free causes have changed, but in their own area, not in that of the mechanism of nature and also not against the course of nature originally ordered by God."[65] Human beings, endowed with the freedom to act contingently, have in the course of history acted in ways that do not further the redemptive divine decree. Human agency has caused changes within the inner circle of the interconnected process of nature but has not had any impact either on the natural laws as divinely ordained for the world nor on the trajectory toward the reign of God: the consummation of the decree has always remained on course. Christ's mission is to further the God-consciousness of human beings and, as God's mediator, to restore the damage done by human beings in the world, to the world, and to themselves through their contingent actions. The incarnation has always been part of God's decree of creation and redemption and is not an afterthought, supplement, or attempt at rectifying past misdeeds. Rather, the incarnation is the keystone of creation: "There is only *one* eternal and general divine decree regarding justification of human beings for Christ's sake. This decree, in turn, is the same thing as Christ's mission. . . . [It] is also simply *at one* with that decree regarding creation of the human race."[66]

Christ "mediates all being of God in the world and all revelation of God through the world"[67] by virtue of his own complete God-consciousness. A precondition for this mediation is Christ's sinlessness. In parallel to his entering history without being deduced from history, Christ enters into the corporate life of sinfulness in the world but does not proceed from it. His entry into the world and his peculiar sinless spiritual character "cannot be accounted for based on the content of the circle of human beings to which he belonged. Rather, it can be accounted for based only on the general source of spiritual life through a creative divine act."[68]

Christ's divinity is identified with the constant, complete potency of his God-consciousness. To communicate or impart his perfect God-consciousness to human beings is the goal of redemption. For this goal to be achievable, human beings must be endowed with both the need for redemption and the potential to receive redemption. Both aspects are

inalienable characteristics of being human and indeed of the original perfection of human nature. Thus, in the context of soteriology, too, creation
and preservation are closely connected. Even though God's activity in
Christ may be regarded as particular, it has universal significance for the
empirical world in which this agency takes place. Likewise, the particular
agency of the Holy Spirit can be understood only within the framework of
universal significance.

For Schleiermacher, the appearance of Christ is itself to be viewed as
preservation, in that it relates to the "preservation of the receptivity of
human nature to take up such an absolute strength of God-consciousness
into itself, a receptivity that was implanted in human nature at its very
onset and that has been continually developing since then."[69] Even though
human nature was incomplete at the first creation of the human race, the
appearance of the Redeemer for the purpose of new creation was already
implanted in it before the time was ripe for the incarnation. Divine providence decrees not only the creation of human beings with the need for and
the capacity to receive redemption, but also the ultimate redemption of all
human beings, even if redemption were to come about only after death.[70]

The work of Christ acts as "the catalyst by which the capacities inherent to human nature may first attain fulfillment."[71] When his activity
establishes itself in an individual, it also becomes person-forming in that
person: "all the individual's activities are then determined differently
through the effect of Christ in the individual."[72] One of the areas in which
this new life in Christ takes shape, although this could not have been
foreseen by Schleiermacher, is ecological living. To act in ways that will
restore and sustain quality of life on earth for future generations chimes
perfectly with the effect of Christ's work of redemption in human beings.
According to Schleiermacher, Christ's work consists in assuming human
beings into the power of his perfect God-consciousness. For those thus
redeemed, being increasingly filled with God-consciousness means that
their free actions increasingly further the divine decree to bring about the
original destiny of human beings and the world. One aspect of this new
life consists in acting in ways that ensure the environmental health of the
planet to sustain future generations for the progression of Christ's work of
redemption. The good deeds performed by the redeemed are in this sense
natural effects of Christ's work of redemption.

The regeneration of a human being from the perspective of a changed
life and the change in a person's relation to God happen simultaneously.
Redemption entails personal transformation toward acts of love relating both to other human beings and to creation. Love seeks to unite with
others. This is equally true of divine and of human love. Granted that
divine attributes are impossible to represent without anthropomorphizing, Schleiermacher asserts that God's love can be posited as the divine

attribute that underpins the ultimate goal of the divine governance of the world, which is redemption and the establishment of the reign of God. This happens through the union of God with human nature in and through Christ. Human nature is created for the one purpose of the self-communicating God whose disposition is love.

CONCLUSION

Schleiermacher's concept of providence takes into account divine and human agency, the interconnected process of nature that implies the relative freedom and absolute dependence of finite agents, and the trajectory of the whole of creation toward redemption:

> The concept of preservation gains its full content only in relation to that element which becomes for us consciousness of grace, leading thereby to the concept of divine causality. Hence, we may say that both processes . . . , the nature of things in their relation to each other and the ordering of their reciprocal influences on each other, subsist by God, just as they subsist in relation to the redemptive revelation of God in Christ or in relation to that revelation of God in Christ which the Spirit is developing toward its consummation.[73]

Human beings, acting and reacting freely within the divinely ordained interconnected process of nature, are part of the single decree to create, sustain, and redeem, and as such are called upon to further the reign of God toward its ultimate consummation. Divine providence therefore implies that human beings act toward sustaining the planet and weave ecological, sustainable living into Christian existence. Schleiermacher's understanding of divine providence, though produced in another time, can encourage Christian efforts to heal the global environmental crisis and to sustain a better life for all humans, who now live in the same global neighborhood.

5

SOCIAL SIN AND THE CULTIVATION
OF NATURE

Kevin M. Vander Schel

In an Advent sermon on the theme of Christ as liberator, Schleiermacher describes the central aspect of Christ's life as consisting neither in his teaching and example nor in his miraculous power over nature, but in the truth "that now Christ is in us as the effective power of our life."[1] In Christ is given the unity and animating center of the common Christian life, and "our goal and aspiration consist solely in furthering the work which God sent him into the world to accomplish, and everything else must relate to this purpose."[2] This homiletic insight underscores a broader theme running throughout Schleiermacher's mature theological writings. The redemption that forms the Christian hope is not a liberation that rescues human beings from the natural bounds of earthly and finite life.[3] Rather, as he writes elsewhere, the natural world itself "is glorified through the life of the Redeemer and hallowed through the efficacy of his Spirit to an unending development of all that is good and godly."[4] As the previous three chapters have described, the redemptive activity of God, rooted in divine providence and manifested in Christ and the Spirit, extends to the whole interconnected process of nature and brings the original perfection of the created world to its proper completion. However, as Schleiermacher likewise notes, both "the glory of the Redeemer" and the particular relationship in which we stand to him are intertwined with "the sinfulness of the human race."[5] While in its original perfection the created and natural world remains open to the coming reign of God, it is everywhere also stamped and misshapen by the pervasive force of sin.

Though Schleiermacher is often charged with holding an overly optimistic or Pelagian view of human progress and society,[6] the awareness of the inescapable derangement or "distortion" (*Störung*) of human nature through sin plays an enduring role in his theological work.[7] The description of distinctively Christian piety in his *Christian Faith* begins with the antithesis between sin and grace, and sets out an account of the intractable and ubiquitous influence of sin in human living. Whether as individuals or in community, Schleiermacher insists, human beings can never fully refrain from sin. To the contrary, "sin creeps into everything."[8] This power of sin is not an independent reality that could be treated in isolation, nor is it a particular feature of Christian experience that could be cleanly separated from other aspects of Christian life. Rather, sin emerges as a lingering opposition to grace in Christian self-consciousness, as an active resistance and persistent "turning away" (*Abwendung*) from God that continually accompanies conscious human living.[9]

Schleiermacher's unique treatment of the doctrine of sin is further distinguished by its unmistakably social character. He presents the universality of sin neither as the result of a tragic historical misstep, as in the Genesis account of the transgression of Adam and Eve, nor as the consequence of an ancient defect or alteration of human nature. Instead, he makes clear that "sinfulness is of a thoroughly collective nature" and insists that it is only in grasping this genuinely social dimension that the notion of sin is properly understood.[10] The state of sin is not primarily a malformation of individual desiring, but a socially mediated and inherently collective condition that everywhere imprints and distorts communal human action. Accordingly, the consequences of sin also have a decidedly social cast. Beyond distortions in individual living, human sinfulness disfigures wider social institutions, cultural movements, and even the natural world.

This novel conception of sin holds important implications for the present challenges of ecological living. While contemporary themes of climate change and ecological impact naturally fell outside the immediate concerns of his own context, Schleiermacher's account nonetheless offers significant resources for conceiving the challenges stemming from ecological devastation as a product of social sin. On the basis of this view, the degradation of the planet does not signal a natural misfortune, an accident of finitude, or an instance of divine wrath but proceeds as an effect of sin, a complex social evil resulting from the cumulative and ongoing entanglement of bias, oversight, and avarice in human communities.

The inherent "commonality" (*Gemeinsamkeit*) of sin also underscores an important aspect of distinctively Christian action in communion with the Redeemer. Corresponding to this extended social conception of sin in Schleiermacher's theology is the pervasive and liberating redemptive activity of God accomplished in Jesus Christ and the Holy Spirit. Just as "sin is essentially something communal,"[11] whose effects reach even to the distortion of the natural and created world, so too the transforming work of the Redeemer extends to all aspects of communal human living. Redemption signals the gradual but decisive transformation of human living through the transition from the collective life of sin to the corporate life of grace. Significantly, then, this activity works a change that reaches beyond the disposition of individual persons and extends fully to the tasks and aims of human society, a theme described in Schleiermacher's lectures on *Christian Ethics* under the heading of the "process of the cultivation of nature" (*Naturbildungsprozeß*). Here the discerning stewardship and care for nature are not derivative or marginal tasks in the Christian life but coextensive with the formation of Christian living overall, as vocations that aim to restore and complete the created world. In the liberation from the captivity of sin, human beings are not redeemed apart from the natural world but only together with it.

This chapter aims to indicate the promise of Schleiermacher's understandings of social sin and the cultivation of nature for contemporary discussions of Christian ecological living. In the liberation from the collective captivity of sin through the redeeming and reconciling activity of Christ, Christian communities are called not to despise the natural world but to find their home within it, as redeemed Christian living plays out in the ongoing care and discerning development of the earth. Developing this position, however, requires first attending to Schleiermacher's innovative revisions of the teachings of sin and evil.

THE SOCIAL DIMENSION OF ORIGINAL AND ACTUAL SIN

The doctrine of sin has exercised a subtle but important role in recent discussions of Christian faith and ecological living. For many critics of the traditional accounts of original sin, the stern focus on sin and salvation in Western theology in the wake of Augustine leads almost invariably to the disparaging of bodily or earthly existence, ushering in an artificial isolation of spiritual life from the natural world and encouraging a dualistic understanding of humanity and nature.[12] On such a view, human beings, while exercising mastery over nature, do not themselves form part of the natural world but find their true citizenship in heaven.[13] By consequence, nature in all its beauty and grandeur is reduced to an arena in which individuals are called to work out their salvation in fear and trembling. The Dominican theologian Matthew Fox, for example, in an updated preface to his ecologically minded work *Original Blessing*, cites the need "to deconstruct the woefully anthropocentric and pessimistic Fall/Redemption religion that begins with 'original sin'" and to establish in its place a spirituality anchored in an affirmation of the "original goodness" of creation.[14] The first step toward an ecologically responsible theology, it would thus seem, is to turn aside from the preoccupying focus on sin and salvation.

While retaining a decidedly Reformed emphasis on the ubiquity of human sinfulness and the priority of grace, Schleiermacher's own treatment differs notably from such privatized and dualistic accounts of sin and salvation and sets forth a significant revision of the customary Augustinian emphases concerning the transmission and expression of original sin.[15] For Schleiermacher, the notion of sin within Christian theology is heuristic. While the constraint of religious feeling and need for redemption are exhibited throughout human living, sin is not properly known in and through itself alone, nor does one arrive at a knowledge of human sin or radical evil through a generalized analysis of natural piety.[16] The doctrine of sin arises from reflection upon the unique character of Christian faith, in its relation with the unique consciousness of grace that marks the fellowship with the Redeemer. This opposition of sin and grace forms the focus of Schleiermacher's depiction of piety in his *Christian Faith* and reflects the enduring conflict that distinguishes Christian living throughout:

> Thus, what is distinctive in Christian piety consists in the following. We are conscious that whatever turning away [*Abwendung*] from God might exist in the situations of our lives is a deed originating in ourselves, and we call this *sin*. However, we are conscious that whatever communion [*Gemeinschaft*] with God might exist there rests upon a communication from the Redeemer, and we call this *grace*.[17]

Schleiermacher furthermore distances his account from any speculative attempt to identify a first origin or cause of human sinfulness in a particular historical moment or natural process. He rejects the manifold variations of the Manichean position that would trace the beginnings of sin and evil to an independently existing reality or principle, whether conceived as physical matter itself or as a separate power of will that might be opposed to God.[18] Likewise, for Schleiermacher, the ubiquity of sin cannot be explained by simple recourse to the biblical narrative of humanity's primordial fall in the garden. The transgression of the first human beings, Adam and Eve, as the "firstfruits of being sinful" (*Erstlinge der Sündigkeit*), instead indicates a subtler truth, illustrating in dramatic fashion the manner in which sin inescapably arises in all.[19] In concrete historical living, each is found already hampered by an inner susceptibility and readiness to sin that exist prior to any particular form of action. Over against the developing awareness of God in human living is the unruly activity of the sensory functions that develop in irregular and disordered fashion to form an increasingly habitual resistance to the unifying and integrating operations of consciousness. Thus, in each "a living seed of sin exists that is constantly at the point of bursting forth" and that forms an active resistance to the consciousness of God as soon as it is awakened by a suitable occasion or outward temptation.[20] While the consciousness of God is never fully extinguished by this constraint, still Schleiermacher maintains that outside the redemptive influence of Christ this "general, original susceptibility to sin" prevails as the "general condition of human beings."[21]

Though it takes root in all, however, this state of sin extends beyond a mere distortion of individual desire. The inescapable tendency to sin, Schleiermacher notes, is mediated historically; it is entrenched in the successive unfolding of social living from generation to generation. The sinful condition of human beings is grounded "somewhere beyond our own individual existence," as each is born into communities and forms of social living already long fractured by the workings of sin.[22] In this manner, the true character of the reign of sin is not to be grasped in the aberrant dispositions, choices, or activities of isolated persons but in the reciprocal and collective life of human beings overall: "in each individual susceptibility to sin is the work of all, and in all individuals it is the work of each."[23]

This social dimension of sin entails a significant reformulation of the traditional categories of original and actual sin. Schleiermacher describes original sin (*Erbsünde*) in novel fashion, as "the collective act [*Gesamttat*] and collective fault [*Gesamtschuld*] of the human race."[24] It indicates the enduring sinful condition in the acting subject, which forms the ground of all specific sinful acts, as "something received and brought along prior to any deed."[25] Such "susceptibility to sin from birth" (*mitgeborene Sündhaftigkeit*) marks an inborn tendency underlying all particular sinful deeds and an abiding inward basis from which the expression of actual sin inevitably proceeds.[26] And as the expression of sin gradually increases and acquires the force of habit, one succumbs to sin "almost irresistibly," giving rise to further sins both in oneself and in others.[27] In "the entire domain of sinful humanity," Schleiermacher notes, one finds no purely good action or moment which is not also mixed together in some fashion with "some hidden contradiction" to the consciousness of God.[28]

Yet due to its collective character, original sin has its proper form not in particular individuals but in the shared reciprocal life of human communities. The shape of sin in any single individual's life is not formed in isolation but reacts to and is complemented by the sin of others, as a participation in the prevailing sinfulness in one's broader sphere of life. The sway of sin is operative in the full network of human relationships and the interconnected life of human communities. It is a "collective power of the flesh" that develops through the interactions and conflicts that define and divide groups over generations and finds expression in the cumulative activities and attitudes that separate persons by family, class, race, and nation. The focus of sin, then, falls not upon individual moral failings or the distortions in one's personal living that flow from misdirected or wayward desires. Rather, the rise of sin in each individual is an instantiation of the sin of larger communities and ultimately of the entire human race: "the susceptibility to sin of each individual refers back to the collective susceptibility to sin of all."[29]

NATURAL AND SOCIAL EVIL

This refashioned account of the universality and inevitability of sin in human social living also introduces an important revision of the relationship between sin and evil. Schleiermacher acknowledges the link between sin and evil as a characteristic feature of distinctively Christian piety, and one that holds a central place in the teachings of original and actual sin. Yet he rejects any position that would ascribe the existence of evil to a fault in the original constitution of the world, according to which evil can be said to precede or provide a prior occasion for the rise of sin. To the contrary, one can properly speak of evil in the world only in connection with human freedom and action, as the product and consequence that follow upon the workings of sin. Apart from sin, Schleiermacher notes, nothing in the transitory and finite world could rightly be considered an evil. The various obstructions and hindrances to life instead would only provide further incentive to consciousness of God and opportunities for more varied expressions of piety.[30] Once given the presence of sin, however, the growth of evil in the world inevitably follows. Where sin is manifest in human beings, one also finds evil in the world.[31]

In this manner, Schleiermacher argues that the customary relation of sin and evil, according to which the prior existence of evil gives rise to sin in human beings, must be reversed: "sin is, above all and overall, the first and original feature, but evil is the derived and secondary feature."[32] Evil is not the cause of sin in human beings but rather names the distortion and deterioration of human living that follows from sin. Thus the presence and growth of evil in the world is inseparably bound to the emergence of sin, and where the pervasive force of sin reigns in human living, the spread of evil follows without fail: "evil is first introduced with the advent of sin, but once sin has appeared it arises inevitably."[33]

Schleiermacher distinguishes two classes of evils that afflict human living in the wake of sin. On one hand, evils emerge not through any actual change in one's life or circumstance but simply because "the world with sin appears to be different to human beings than it would have seemed without it."[34] Bodily afflictions and physical inhibitions that in themselves are not intrinsically opposed to the consciousness of God—such as weakness, scarcity, disease, or even bodily death—are now reckoned as miseries that beset and torment human life. In the light of sin, these unavoidable hindrances to life, which are independent of human action, are reckoned as a kind of "natural evil" (*natürliches Übel*) that afflicts all persons. On the other hand, however, a further class of troubles and sorrows in life proceeds expressly from human actions. Such "social evil" (*geselliges Übel*) arises from the ongoing conflict and opposition between human beings, from oppressive and antagonistic action and the virtually innumerable ways in which persons and communities hinder, injure, and suppress others in pursuit of some private interest or concern.[35] These social injustices often yield clear and immediate effects, such as violence, destruction, alienation, abuse, and exploitation. They also exercise an ongoing impact upon future generations, shaping and misshaping social structures, cultural traditions, and political and civic institutions.

Accordingly, when considering the question of the affliction of evils as punishment for sin, Schleiermacher departs from the view that would attribute the various punishments of sin to the righteous wrath of God. He affirms that all evil, when viewed in its connection with divine causality, "is to be regarded as punishment [*Strafe*] for sin."[36] Yet it forms such a punishment in the limited sense that evil enters the world as the inescapable by-product and consequence of human sin. Natural evils reflect this penalty only indirectly, as in the wake of sin the natural imperfections, pain, and the limitations of finite existence itself are experienced as evil. Social evils, by contrast, exhibit the punishment for sin in more direct and lasting fashion, through the expanding and deepening "deterioration of the world" (*Verschlimmerung der Welt*) that follows from communal human sin.[37]

In this respect, then, the growth of evil in the world depends upon and corresponds to the increase of sin in human living, such that "as sin decreases, evil would also decrease."[38] Schleiermacher cautions, however, against an overly narrow or simplistic reading of this connection between evil and sin, by means of which one might attribute the evils afflicting particular persons or communities to some divinely ordained punishment for their specific sins. Evil is instead the "collective punishment" (*Gesamtstrafe*) consequent to the "collective fault" (*Gesamtschuld*) of sin.[39] Not only do children suffer for the sins of their parents, but all persons suffer for the sins of others.[40]

SCHLEIERMACHER AND ECOLOGICAL SIN

Schleiermacher's emphasis on the inherently social character of sin sets his treatment apart from more customary Augustinian accounts of original and actual sin, and it introduces an important shift in modern theological discussions of sin and society.[41] Though at times criticized for its seemingly subjectivist approach to sin, Schleiermacher's revision of the doctrine marks an important departure from privatized and reductive accounts of human sinfulness. He presents sin not merely as an inward feature of individual Christian piety that comes to the fore in one's particular acts but as a collective distortion of human living whose ongoing effects become ossified in cultural practices, social movements, and political institutions. As such, his treatment significantly anticipates the important critical analyses of structural sin and structural violence developed more recently by liberation and feminist theologians.[42]

This conception of social sin, together with the distinction between natural and social evil, also holds notable promise for drawing out the ecological ramifications of the Christian doctrine of sin.[43] Beyond its interior existential dimension, human sinfulness marks a collective turning away from God, a malformation of human living structurally embedded in social and cultural institutions, which both distorts communal human action and reshapes the surrounding environment. And its impact extends not only to consequences of specific wrongdoings or moral failings but also to pervasive and deeply rooted cycles of decline and exploitation.

Where then do environmental devastation and the abuse of natural resources fit into this scheme of sin and redemption? At first glance the deterioration of the planet might appear to be a species of natural evil. In contrast to the immense suffering and injury caused by the devastations of war, political oppression, or socioeconomic injustice, such ecological degradation would seem to simply reflect the limits of created finitude, an unavoidable aspect of the constant—and often immensely destructive— flux of the finite physical world manifested in natural disasters such as storms, floods, earthquakes, and volcanic eruptions. For human beings, the natural world is a place of beauty and abundance but also of thorns and thistles, toil and hardship (Gen. 3:18–19). In some respects, nature will always remain wild and dangerous, and in spite of all best efforts, pain, loss, and sickness are bound to continue in the natural world. Yet in following Schleiermacher's own unique scheme, the destruction and suffering caused by the deterioration of the earth more closely corresponds to the category of social evil. It proceeds as a product and consequence of the distortions of collective human action, as the natural world is damaged and misshapen by human wrongdoing. It thus forms an important and far-reaching manifestation of the consequences of human sin, the result of long-standing patterns of domination and exploitation of the natural environment.

This ecological dimension of human sinfulness provides a helpful lens for illuminating ongoing aspects of anthropogenic environmental devastation. Human-induced threats to the planet are well documented, and concrete examples of the exploitation of nature are distressingly easy to come by. In addition to the disastrous consequences of global warming, these include systematic deforestation, pollution caused by industrial waste, the increasing salinization of oceans, and the destruction of natural habitats and species, with short- and long-term consequences both for existing ecosystems and the ongoing health of human communities.

In some cases the human actions behind environmental destruction are clear and direct. One such example is the recent discovery of oceanic "garbage patches," sprawling collections of plastics, discarded fishing nets, and marine debris that have appeared in the world's major oceans.[44] A majority of this waste is composed of synthetic polymers, from items such as plastic bags or food and beverage containers, which decompose only slowly and incompletely if at all.[45] This debris in turn harms marine life and interrupts ecosystems, affecting plankton and algae as well as larger marine animals such as tuna, sea turtles, seals, and albatrosses. Moreover, these marine plastics have the potential to impact human health as they enter the food chain.[46]

A parallel problem exists with the disposal of e-waste. As discarded laptops, smartphones, and other electronic products are broken down or decay, they release toxic chemicals such as lead, cadmium, and polyvinyl chloride into the ground and air. According to United Nations estimates, roughly twenty million to fifty million tons of electronics are discarded per year, with many developed countries, such as the United States, exporting their electronic waste to disposal sites in China, India, and developing West African nations, where workers often dismantle these products without adequate protective clothing, endangering their own health and the health of surrounding communities.[47] In both of these cases, ecological devastation is not the effect of natural processes but the result of increasing economic and technological consumption and excessive human waste.

The social and ecological conception of sin also offers insight into those cases of planetary degradation in which human involvement is more complicated and indirect. Descriptions of the Dust Bowl and the series of dust storms that afflicted the southern Great Plains throughout the 1930s tell of immense waves of dust and sand that choked crops, killed livestock, took lives of young children and the elderly, and dislocated families.[48] Personal accounts from the time depict these "black blizzards" in striking and often apocalyptic language. Terrifying waves of dust towering thousands of feet high, crackling with static electricity, often obscured the sun for days and brought plagues of jackrabbits and grasshoppers in their wake.[49] To some, these powerful storms were simply a natural disaster, an unmanageable and destructive expression of the fundamental economy of nature. Others saw in them a sign of divine judgment or even a herald of the "end of the world."[50] Yet in addition to the natural factors of wind and weather—droughts had occurred in the region for centuries, and the area is particularly susceptible to wind erosion—the onslaught of storms was made possible by the introduction of unsustainable and short-sighted agricultural practices intended to transform the native grasslands into more profitable cropland.

Lured by land developers who promised that "rain follows the plow," farmers and homesteaders, who were frequently persons of "slender means," rapidly settled in the southern Great Plains area.[51] Utilizing advances in agricultural technology that allowed more efficient plowing and harvesting, they quickly began removing native drought-resistant buffalo and grama grasses that protected the soil in favor of cash crops such as wheat. The economic collapse and desperation of the Great Depression in the early 1930s only hastened these efforts, as farmers rushed to plant more crops to offset the drop in prices.[52] Unable to withstand the region's periodic drought and severe winds, soil from these shallow fields would be taken up and carried for hundreds of miles, contributing to a cycle of increasing devastation in the grasslands. In this manner, the ecological crisis in the southern Great Plains, while not brought about deliberately or with malicious intent, nonetheless owed its emergence in large part to human oversight, as the outcome of a slow accumulation of irresponsible practices, poor judgment, and avarice.

Even suffering caused by genuinely natural disasters, such as the deadly 2004 Indian Ocean tsunami, cannot be easily disentangled from the effects of sin. The massive earthquake off the coast of Sumatra, along with the immensely destructive waves that followed, were due to no discernible human actions, and indeed follow a cycle of seismic activity that predates human cultures by hundreds of thousands of years.[53] Still, the loss of life that followed cannot be so cleanly extricated from human involvement. Among the roughly 230,000 persons estimated to have perished on the coasts of Indonesia, Sri Lanka, India, Thailand, and other surrounding countries were approximately 9,000 foreign tourists. In the aftermath of the disaster, harrowing stories from vacationers, businesspeople, and diplomats who survived were recounted in internationally syndicated columns, captured in amateur video recordings later broadcast on social media, and—at least in one case—dramatically re-created in a major motion picture.[54] However, the majority of the dead, as well as the millions of others who were displaced, were from poorer local communities, and many had been recently forced from areas of conflict and political instability to reorganize their lives and livelihood around the shorelines.[55] Furthermore, reports in the aftermath of the disaster estimated that a disproportionate number of the dead were children, and that in affected areas of Indonesia, Sri Lanka, and India four times as many women as men lost their lives.[56] Taken in isolation, the occurrence of an earthquake may be regarded a simple phenomenon of nature. That so many were left vulnerable and unprotected, however, points to wider and long-standing failings in social practices and structures.

These examples of environmental exploitation serve to highlight an important aspect of Schleiermacher's conception of sin and evil. While natural evil is everywhere present in human experience, it is in practice difficult to isolate or separate from the reach of social evil.[57] Sickness, lack of medicine or adequate health care, hunger, and loss play out amid an intricate web of interpersonal relations, social structures, and cultural institutions. And on every side, the anxiety of human finitude and the sting of death are bounded by the shortcomings of particular human communities. Moreover, as the above examples make clear, the burden of these threats falls disproportionately on those who are poor and marginalized in their own societies and in the international community. As Schleiermacher notes, the greatest perpetrators of sin are rarely the ones to most keenly suffer its effects.[58]

THE CULTIVATION OF NATURE

As the above description indicates, Schleiermacher's novel treatment of social sin frames a far-reaching and comprehensive account of human sinfulness. Yet this collective character and expansive scope of sin and evil find their counterpart in the communication of grace. As the "collective life [Gesamtleben] of sin" is the collective act of human beings, it is overcome only in the communal life of grace grounded in the efficacious activity of Christ, which likewise extends to the entirety of the human race.[59] This new and "divinely wrought collective life" that proceeds from Christ yields a transition from the misery of sin to the blessedness of communion with God.[60] The entrance of Christ into humanity inaugurates the dawning reign of God in human history, signaling both the passage from this sinful condition and the coming completion of the created world.[61]

Schleiermacher describes the communication of grace in the influence of the Redeemer under the central soteriological categories of regeneration and sanctification. His Christian Faith describes regeneration as the decisive turning point in personal living and the emergence of a new form of life. In the union with Christ, "one's life stands under a different formulation and is consequently a new life."[62] This change of heart yields the beginning of a new personality grounded in faith and a thoroughgoing regret for sin. Sanctification, in turn, denotes the further development of this new life in the cultivation of the human person's "natural forces" and activity for the reign of God, the ongoing expansion of a new "mode of life."[63] In the founding of this "new collective life," whose fruits are good works, human living grows increasingly attuned to the divine will, and the power of sin progressively weakens and disappears.[64] This important theme of the unfolding of sanctification in the natural and historical world receives its fullest treatment, however, not in Schleiermacher's *Christian Faith* but in his lectures on Christian ethics, which consider the forms and tasks of distinctively Christian action.[65]

No less than his *Christian Faith*, Schleiermacher's *Christian Ethics* turns upon the "great contradiction" (*großer Widerspruch*) of sin and grace in human living.[66] His lectures on Christian ethics set forth no competing theoretical accounts of the doctrines of sin and grace but rather extend and complement the treatments of his *Glaubenslehre* by analyzing the relation of sin and grace to the various modes and activities of historical human communities. Schleiermacher organizes his treatment of Christian ethics around three central and interrelated forms of distinctively Christian action.[67] The first, presentational or representational action (*darstellendes Handeln*), works no specific change on the outer world but expresses the inward blessedness and communion with God that anchor the Christian community's identity and vocation. Together with this foundational dimension of Christian action, Schleiermacher also distinguishes two forms of efficacious action: purifying (*reinigende*) and broadening or propagative (*verbreitende*) action. Purifying action reflects the variety of corrective activities directed against the "force of sin" (*Gewalt der Sünde*) and designed to counter the existing effects and consequences of sin.[68] Broadening action, by contrast, signals the positive growth or expansion of the influence of Christ and the Spirit over the entirety of the natural and created world.

The awareness of the pervasive effects of sin and the stubborn existence of evil in culture and society is an ever-present feature of the lectures on Christian ethics. Accordingly, purifying action, which proceeds from the consciousness of sin, is wide-ranging and comprehensive in scope, laboring to remedy diseased or distorted traditions, customs, and social structures that have developed both inside and outside the church. Such action has a prophetic and reformative character, aiming to amend and rehabilitate wayward cultural practices and fragmented social institutions, and Schleiermacher's lectures make clear that the need for this work is ongoing and will continue until the final consummation of God's reign.[69]

The focus of Schleiermacher's Christian ethics, however, falls on the expanding influence of Christ and the Spirit over the natural and historical world. This broadening dimension of Christian living, proceeding from the consciousness of grace, concerns the dual cultivation of the inward Christian "disposition" (*Gesinnung*) and outer Christian "talents" (*Talente*) and corresponds to the treatment of regeneration and sanctification in Schleiermacher's *Christian Faith*.[70] The cultivation of disposition reflects the widening growth of the Christian community and signals the reality of conversion by divine grace, the new "birth" (*Geburt*) that is "life stepping into the light," as through communion with Christ the Spirit becomes the active and unifying principle in the life of the human being.[71] Together with this new unity of life is a progressive formation of human capacities, functions, and skills to bring them into greater conformity with the leading of the Spirit. This continuing growth and extension of human activity constitutes the development of Christian "virtue" (*Tugend*) or talent, and it designates the sanctification of human living through the increasing rule of the Spirit over the positive tasks and outward activities of human living.[72]

This twofold cultivation of disposition and talent provides the basis for Schleiermacher's analysis of the expansion of the Spirit's influence over the social, cultural, and political spheres of human action. It also carries important insights into the relation of human beings to the natural world. The divine activity that proceeds from Christ and endures in the Holy Spirit does not operate magically in the world, as if interrupting human history from above, but transforms the natural and created world from within, appropriating and critically modifying existing modes and structures of human activity.[73] The cultivation of Christian disposition thus ties into already developed forms of family life and social community. The cultivation of Christian talent, by contrast, draws upon a variety of activities through which human beings engage their environment, a wide and comprehensive range of action Schleiermacher describes as the "process of the cultivation of nature" (*Naturbildungsprozeß*).

This progressing cultivation of nature, in Schleiermacher's conception, encompasses all the practices and activities through which individuals and communities engage the external world, the "entire earthly activity [*irdische Thätigkeit*] of the human person."[74] It indicates the intentional and volitional development of nature by human beings, as societies labor to shape and organize their natural environment. As such, this cooperative process indicates the overarching "vocation of the human being on earth" (*Beruf des Menschen auf der Erde*), highlighting the moral task of guiding and shepherding the cultivation of nature through human power and skill.[75]

Within this context, Schleiermacher's lectures describe the training and formation of human capacities and practices, along with their corresponding social and cultural goods. This broad range of activity thus concerns productive human action in all its various modes, such as the differentiation of labor, economic exchange, the organization of civil society, the establishment of laws, and the formation of the state. At times, the lectures speak of this overarching activity in terms of the human governance or "mastery" over nature, alluding to the language of the authority and "dominion" granted to Adam and Eve in the garden (Gen. 1:27–28).[76] But the cultivation of nature in Schleiermacher's Christian ethics provides a substantially different lens for considering the human relationship to the natural world. It does not condone the manipulation or despoiling of the natural world for technological, economic, or political ends, nor does it correspond to Albrecht Ritschl's conception of the Christian's "positive world-dominating freedom."[77] Rather, it denotes the care for and discerning cultivation of the created and natural world as an intrinsic feature of sanctification in the Christian community. Indeed, Schleiermacher argues, the formation of virtuous human talents and the responsible cultivation of the natural world should not be considered separate tasks but rather dual aspects of the growing process of sanctification. In a pair of lecture notes from 1809, he writes, "The cultivation of talent [*Bildung des Talentes*] and the cultivation of nature through talent [*Bildung der Natur durch das Talent*] is one and the same function"; there is an "original identity [*Identität*] of cultivation of talent and cultivation of nature."[78]

Accordingly, the depiction of the developing Christian life in Schleiermacher's Christian ethics offers an important contrast to dualistic or ahistorical spiritual attitudes that emphasize the alienation of human beings from natural and earthly existence. In growing conformity with the will of Christ and the leading of the Spirit, Christian communities are called not to withdraw from the natural world but to become at home within it.[79] As that part of the interconnected natural order that has become conscious of the utter dependence of all finite existence upon God, human persons are tasked with shepherding the natural and created world toward its completion in the reign of God. In this respect, Schleiermacher's lectures on Christian ethics develop an important insight in the Reformed tradition, which recognizes the tasks of stewardship and care for the natural creation as a central part of the Christian life.[80]

Furthermore, within Christian communities, care for the cultivation of nature also includes an important process of critical discernment. In communion with Christ the various existing aspects of human activity in and toward the natural world are not to be merely accepted but must be continually reformed, modified, and restored. From the Christian standpoint, current structures of social and political living, forms of economic development, and cultural and technical achievements may neither be considered inevitable nor complete; instead, each should be regarded merely as a "point of transition" (*Durchgangspunkt*) in the ongoing historical development of the reign of God.[81] Schleiermacher's treatment thus underscores the need for ongoing reflection upon the various tasks and challenges of human engagement with the natural world and portrays the communal Christian life as a continuing search for ever more adequate forms of living in and with the created world.

CONCLUSION: REDEMPTION OF THE NATURAL WORLD

This brief overview of Schleiermacher's conceptions of social sin and the cultivation of nature suggests a novel perspective on present ecological challenges and offers an important contribution to contemporary theological discussions of planetary living. Drawing upon the insights of Schleiermacher's unique understanding of sin and redemption, the degradation of the earth, together with its consequences for existing ecosystems and human communities, appears neither as a mere consequence of natural finitude nor an unavoidable by-product of the economy of nature but as an evil rooted in the collective turning away from God. Correspondingly, the responsible development of redeemed Christian living does not entail a separation from nature but plays out in constant care for and cultivation of the natural world.

In view of some common interpretations of Schleiermacher's theological legacy, such a perspective may contain a number of surprising elements. In locating piety in immediate self-consciousness and "the feeling of absolute dependence," Schleiermacher is often numbered among those thinkers who reduce the complex realities and tensions of Christian living to merely inward and subjective features of religious experience, and whose theology consequently encourages a "personalist reduction of the scope of salvation" that leaves little room for meeting pressing ecological challenges and concerns.[82] Yet Schleiermacher's historically minded analysis of Christian living stands in notable contrast to this privatized view. His *Christian Faith* and lectures on Christian ethics portray human sinfulness not simply as an internal feature of Christian self-consciousness but as a complex and socially mediated reality that is enmeshed and embedded in the developing institutions and structures of human societies. Likewise, within Schleiermacher's mature theology, the redemptive work of Christ not only yields a transformation of personal living but also inaugurates a renewal of creation, ushering in the fulfillment and completion of the natural and historical world in the reign of God.

Schleiermacher's social understanding of sin and redemption also involves a substantial reorientation in Christian attitudes toward suffering and evil in the natural world. His treatment depicts the devastation of nature and the evils that plague human communities not as reprisals for violations of divine law but as destructive consequences that follow upon collective human sin. Far from a punitive outpouring of divine wrath, the evils that afflict human living and threaten the planet are the fruits of distorted human action, and the alleviation of this suffering awaits the growing influence of the redemptive activity of Christ and the Spirit in the natural world.

In this fashion, Schleiermacher's thought outlines notable if often neglected resources for reinvestigating the Christian tradition in light of ecological concerns and for drawing out the ecological ramifications of central Christian doctrines. His theology thus provides an important complement to larger currents in contemporary theological conversations of ecological living. Attention to the centrality of ecojustice in Christian living has been a steadily increasing emphasis of Orthodox, Catholic, and Protestant theology alike. Numerous Orthodox theologians and bishops, including Ecumenical Patriarch Bartholomew, have underscored the rich interconnections of the environment with themes of nature, creation, and deification in the patristic tradition.[83] Similarly, a growing number of Roman Catholic theologians have highlighted the centrality of environmental concerns to Catholic thought and praxis, and the growing ecological crisis is the theme of Pope Francis's 2015 papal encyclical *Laudato Si'*.[84] Reformed theologians have likewise contributed significant resources to this discussion, with recent studies critically recovering and developing important insights from key figures such as Karl Barth, Jürgen Moltmann, and Colin Gunton.[85] These combined studies provide a broad basis for the renewal and rediscovery of the wisdom of the Christian tradition in the face of the challenges of the ecological crisis and signal the insight that true Christian practice cannot be separated from responsible planetary living.

Amid this larger chorus of voices, however, Schleiermacher's theology retains an important place. His theology illuminates the relation of ecological concerns not only to doctrines of anthropology, creation, and ecclesiology but also to Christianity's soteriological center in the opposition of sin and grace. The reign of God that overcomes the collective power of sin does not liberate human beings from concern with the natural world; on the contrary, the redemption that grounds Christian hope emerges only in and through an ongoing and faithful engagement with nature.

CONCLUSION

Schleiermacher and Ecotheology

Terrence N. Tice

An ecotheology formed strictly on the basis of Schleiermacher's principles would be drawn from precisely those kinds of factors within Schleiermacher's teachings on behalf of the Christian church that have been indicated in the previous five chapters. His theology is especially intended for Christian communities of faith, but it works well in tandem with distinctly different modes of faith. A few poignant ecotheological aspects of his theology may be summed up in the following four ideas: Christ is the Redeemer; Christ's Spirit continues to redeem humanity; humanity is part of the one web of being; and Christians are called to be inclusive, reforming, and in dialogue.[1] I treat each of these ideas in turn, weaving together strands of Schleiermacher's thought that have been discussed in the book to this point.

First, God has made a distinct intervention in the order of creation by sending Christ, by his entire life unto death—but not by his death alone—to redeem the human race from sin. During his life on earth Christ was sinless, perfect, and in a blessed state; thus, he also constantly held within himself a perfect God-consciousness. In conveying that God-consciousness to others, which comprises the process by which God's own divine being is made present in his life, Christ's preparing, converting, justifying, and sanctifying presence is still passed on and preserved in the visible and invisible church. By this same reconciling and redemptive process, God wills to enable other humans to grasp how the entire species is, first, to develop as "children" in relationship with the Creator and Preserver of the universe. Second, as human beings grow in their relationship to one another on this earth—and therefore in proper relation to the entire interconnected process (or ecological mechanism) of nature in which humanity is placed—God will enable humanity to grasp toward what complete end the human species is supernaturally given to attain and is naturally given to receive: spiritual perfection and blessedness in community with Christ.

A second aspect of Schleiermacher's thought that could benefit ecotheology is that, for him, regenerate Christians—who are being sanctified and can never slip back into being nonredeemed creatures—are constantly growing, despite setbacks and constant strife between humanity's more sensory-oriented susceptibility, the sinfulness accrued from earlier generations, and actually sinning themselves, on the one hand; and advancing within Christian religious immediate self-consciousness, on the other hand. Those two conflicting roots of unconscious and conscious life, both individual and collective, are open to correction always by impetus from divine grace in inner faith and thus expressed in thought and action both within human relationships and between human and other life on the planet. Therewith, Christians experience God's Spirit as shared, sacred Holy Spirit—which is different from Christ, to be sure, because it is collective in nature, yet is also at one with that of Christ himself. With others touched by divine preparatory grace, those who have been affected by Christians' predecessors in faith as by mutual religious experiences— whether the participants are living more within inner circles of the church, within outer circles of the church, or wholly outside it—are able to make common cause with one another. This is so by virtue of whatever degree of species-consciousness human beings have attained. In common with the entire species, the Christian church is at work in the mission to which God calls its adherents: to move out into the rest of the world. All finite being, Schleiermacher avers, is absolutely dependent on God. One day human beings will be so in concert with all things. Both internally and externally as God's beloved community in Christ and in Spirit, Christians are enjoined to open themselves to, confess, celebrate, and caringly work on concerns that arise among the rest of humankind, both ecological and ecumenical. Schleiermacher called the various stages of such involvements being in "the household [eco-, ecu-] of God."

Third, on Schleiermacher's platform, crisis denial would be a new great candidate for original sin, passed on to current generations. As actual sinners, humans have always influenced others' patterns of sinning, patterns that they have distinctly adopted and modified. These social sins—in which Christians could readily have been complicit—require acknowledgment, forgiveness, redemption, and moves toward meaningful action, before all else. These activities comprise the ethos of the very personal existence of each in community with Christ, with the common spirit that is Holy Spirit, with our Father/Mother (original Progenitor), and thereby with God. As Christians experience benevolent love from God and are meant to return to God calm acceptance and gratitude, along with an active wish for others to experience this love as well, they also act in relationship to the ecologies that make up the world. The earth is itself one whole; the universe is one whole; both are created and preserved as one reality by God. Whether individual or in some smaller collectivity, humans are, in fact, inseparable from the earth-world, despite efforts to the contrary. Humanity is part of one indivisible web of being.[2]

A poignant fourth aspect of Schleiermacher's theology is that the Christian church, in particular, is to act as part of the one web of being in three special ways: (a) by presenting in word and deed a faithful proclamation of love and efficaciously loving others by gestures of welcoming, accepting others as equals, and including others in their company; (b) by self-purifying, critically assessing, reforming action, which is to be directed first within individual participants and therewith realized in the life of the church, and then, lovingly, in the rest of the world; and (c) by broadening action, appropriate to its calling in life with Christ, action that does not sequester itself, does not harbor pride or triumphalism, does not militate against or do violence to any, but that is in loving and respectful dialogue with all.[3]

These four aspects of Schleiermacher's theology support the formation and use of principles that lend hope to pertinent efforts specifically based on ecotheology, both more physical and more socially human in nature. They also ground efforts to overcome sinful attitudes, values, and action in that regard. The following section, also reflective of his thought and example, points the way to the general perspective that he would have in addressing problems of ecology and sustainability today.

AN ECOTHEOLOGY THAT OFFERS HOPE

Until the contemporary period, human beings have had few grounds, if any, to suppose that we could actually destroy each other and the precious living soil of earth with such devastation as we have already performed. Nor could we dream that we had the power to destroy most of our own kind and of other kinds of life, not so nearly completely as we now actually can. Nor have we been able to suppose that by our own instrumentalities of commerce we could produce global warming by emission of greenhouse gases into the atmosphere with such deleterious effects as they have had. Over the past century, however, the damage done has become so steep and unrelenting that this curve itself must be destroyed and earth turned back to the preindustrial levels of noxious emissions that prevailed in the fourteenth century. Fortunately, this goal can be achieved because of knowledge that has been attained over the same period. A Schleiermacher-inspired ecotheology alone cannot save us. However, it offers hope toward a fully efficacious outcome.

This hope lies in what Schleiermacher calls "the one eternal divine decree of creation and redemption."[4] As Anette Hagan has shown in chapter 4, the whole of Schleiermacher's dogmatic theology can be restated under the concept of providence.[5] Schleiermacher purposely did not choose to use that concept because of speculative elements that have continually been associated with it in previous eras. However, the elements empha-sized in an account of God's providence would contain several key ele-ments also well covered in the current volume taken as a whole. The rest of this subsection, therefore, restates what has been covered heretofore by indicating these key elements arranged in view of what actions Christians are to take in their relation to God's green earth. In grouping the whence and how, the nexus and networks of the elements contained in Schleier-macher's ecotheology are made clear in sharp relief. Hence, how they can be joined to proposals that economists are working on is also put into proper perspective. These elements are thus enumerated here in almost strictly formulaic batches.

1. God's activity in relation to the world of nature is always an inter-connected world-shaping process, including that of human nature. Thus, consciousness of grace is prior to consciousness of sin. All through the Christian life, the "new creation" that Christ was enabled to bring into being presupposes divine activity of grace, which Schleiermacher repeat-edly refers to as "the supernatural becoming natural" in the way it then operates. Human beings receive grace in what the Jesus tradition in the New Testament calls inner "faith" in one's relationship with God. Prepa-ratory grace, inside and outside the church, is still grace. It is a gift that provides impetus to the renewed (redeemed) life of a community that responds to God in faith.

2. In relation to human beings, as we have seen, nature gains free will and, like all life, it has to develop and evolve, individually, in collective form, and as a species.

3. In all this special process, brought to us by Christ, then within a developing and diverse Christian church, with other faith traditions that are responding to divine aspects of what has arisen within their own jour-neys, God takes form as a "common spirit," which the Christian tradi-tion calls Holy Spirit, withal seeing to these matters: that is to say, God is providential.

4. Under God's and each other's care, children go through stages of development, and those who do not die before they grow old all go through what we call "the life cycle" today. Science has advanced some-what beyond what Schleiermacher could say about this, though rather slowly when compared with what physical science can tell us about the tiniest ingredients and about the whole process that makes up the uni-verse. Science itself, as Schleiermacher did anticipate with great vision, has been going through a multistage development since ancient times. It has done this at a very fast pace over the past century but is far from per-fect methodologically as yet. Psychology would address anything that can be seen to go on inside us and because of our own impulses when our lives are transformed and accompanied by forces of impetus. Some of these

forces of impetus a great many humans call God. For Schleiermacher, this God, as revealed to us in Jesus, is not *a being* but Supreme Being, not a "person" or three "persons" but one being acting with personal impact in and alongside persons and yet not performing as if constituted by human-like faculties in Godself. Providence works differently when God presents Godself, as it were, in the divine economy, at home with us and we with God. God sees to things, brings them about, with radical difference, as wholly Other, as One in the all, as one in three economic moves. And yet, God does this also in ways that we can eventually come to *see* with our own minds and hearts.

Schleiermacher's contemporaneity with twenty-first-century people lies in the vision and feeling for the reality we can be led to face and take care of, the challenges we can accept and resolve, the climate and social crisis we have rapidly constructed and must very soon turn completely around.

5. God wills this entire interwoven process of a human earth eter-nally—that is, beyond time and beyond space—which for Schleiermacher means that God, unlike human beings, does what God wills, sees to it, and, within our spatial-temporal domain, has willed what God does, leav-ing room for wickedness and what comes of error, the social evils that God has provided for. The reality that God has created and preserves as an intricate process comes in wholes (ecologies) and is itself a whole (the earth and its atmosphere). The "decree" by which God has ordained this complex whole of wholes is *one*: both creation and new creation in Christ within it. What we experience as natural evils are punishments only because or insofar as they derive from actions or mistakes we have made by our free will. God sees all this and *provides* for how it is all to be handled or governed, within conditions set by God's "government of the world." Naturally, it is often others who most suffer for both wickedness and natural ills that other humans have brought about. We humans can-not see, though we might graphically anticipate, what is to come of such matters or of us, individually or collectively, after our death. Christ inti-mates that he will be with the Father and that as we all continue to grow in faith we will all eventually be one in communion with God; but he stops short of trying to prophesy what humans cannot know but can only hope will comport with what we can now know as God's wisdom and love, in an eternal life for all. We all together bear responsibility for what good or ill occurs on earth. In God's company, all of that which God sees, and sees to, comes to be real for us as well. That is the story regarding divine providence. Its outline comprises the whole story that is available to us in this life.

In sum, these are the principles that Schleiermacher offered, not only in his "dogmatics" (i.e., his teachings on behalf of Christians and their churches) but also in his extensive preaching, academic activity, public and sociopolitical life, and still other activities—all of it in order further to accomplish in other ways the practices that Jesus had instituted or manifested during his own redemptive, mediating, reconciling, popular teaching, governing, and public ministerial or serving activity on earth. For Schleiermacher, Jesus was the sinless, perfect, and blessed prototype for our turning crises—such as global warming—into something like Naomi Klein's new, regenerate, and sustainably developing economy.[6]

Now, a long-standing tradition of Catholic natural apologetic theology has come from Pope Francis, reflecting a contemplative Franciscan tradition. It appeared in his brilliantly formed encyclical supporting concerted efforts to reverse climate change, *Laudato Si'* (2015). This tradition has flourished in streams of Dutch Calvinist and Anglo-American theology, in forms similar to Catholic apologetics.[7] Schleiermacher himself eschews any attempt to defend, prove, or sell Christianity, basing his theological presentations solely on empirical contemplation of "Christian religious immediate self-consciousness." Like John Dewey after him, he attempts to build his theological efforts on strictly empirical psychological grounds— that is, on what can be observed first within and then, interconnectedly, on other observable external experience. Schleiermacher's approach admittedly cannot totally avoid philosophical importations, especially in cognitive frames like "absolute dependence," used both to identify and discuss affective and perceptual experience, but he strove to limit himself to these relatively nonmetaphysical concepts. Schleiermacher eschews apologetic efforts directed outside the church, restricting his preaching to proclamation based on Scripture and to critically realist purifying action directed to the church. In contrast, Pope Francis heavily relies on his onetime Franciscan colleague (a Franciscan until 1992), the philosophically oriented Brazilian theologian Leonardo Boff, who has himself offered two powerful works in ecotheology.[8] Naturally, no single theological work in English carries the global influence that Pope Francis's encyclical does. It is, in itself, an outcry of deep concern.

THE ECONOMIC BASIS OF TODAY'S CRITICAL GLOBAL CHALLENGE

The global challenge that has motivated this book is climate change. The first signs of atmospheric warming had been identified by European physicists in 1908. Since then, those signs have been closely followed by meteorologists and other climate scientists, who have known that they are caused by the emission of greenhouse gases into the atmosphere. These are chiefly carbon dioxide (CO_2) from burning fossil fuels like oil, coal,

and natural gas, and other gases such as methane and other biomass products in much smaller proportions. Thus far, this concluding chapter has
emphasized collective entities and the entire human species. The causes
and effects of climate changes, however, are also quite personal.

To invite identification among other personal stories, I here venture
to risk being charged with getting too personal by sharing features of
my own story. As a Christian, I have known since childhood that, as the
familiar hymn goes, "in Christ there is no east or west . . . but one great
fellowship of love throughout the whole wide earth." I knew then that we
and every living thing are hugely interdependent. In that sense, I took the
popular exclamation "It's a small world!" more and more seriously. At
age fourteen, in late 1945, I wrote an article for a hometown newspaper
warning of the rising nuclear arms race, not realizing then that this dangerous source of energy would soon be harnessed to provide so-called
clean fuel. I had to search out this subject in our rural county library. I had
caught wind of a "nuclear arms race" but had no idea what it was. The
news had not yet penetrated our isolated neck of the woods.

Effects from burning fossil fuels have already devastated life everywhere, especially hidden from sight in the global saltwater seas, which
are full of vulnerable living creatures. At a fast pace, we are destroying
vital reefs, melting down Greenland's massive store of ice, and losing the
polar ice caps. Without abatement of the current pace, vast flooding will
inundate at least twenty-five large cities in coastal areas from just two
inches' rise of those seas, and whole economies will go under water if
this fast-moving trend is not reversed. We humans are nested in our various natural ecologies—earth itself being one integrated "world body," a
small, interdependent, "interconnected process of nature," to use Schleiermacher's words. Today everyone should know, from both natural scientists and social scientists, that everything on this earth is dependent on
everything else. As a theologian, Schleiermacher claimed two centuries
ago that, both currently and ultimately, everything is "absolutely dependent on God," the creator and preserver of the entire universe, to which
fact he as a Christian counseled reaching toward "calm acceptance" and
"gratitude" in our prayers. The earth provides a home for us, as Schleiermacher saw it, which still lives on, precariously, under treaties meant to
hold back the use of nuclear weapons in war.

In 1966, having worked at the World Council of Churches headquarters
in Geneva for three years, I had come to the University of Michigan for
further study. I titled one after-hours evening course The Human Earth, in
which Ann Arbor folk explored with me the humanly inhabited earth and
its problems. This was a year before the first Earth Day. A few years later, I
was meeting with a group of physicists at the University of Michigan who
had much to do with changing US policy regarding use of intercontinental

ballistic missiles (ICBMs), some of which carry nuclear warheads. Despite resulting treaties restricting ICBMs, hundreds and thousands of these missiles still stand ready for use by multiple nations, including North Korea. Today most of us know that this source of power can unleash damage to the earth and its inhabitants that will not go away for hundreds of years.

Today, as Schleiermacher acknowledged, humans are still created so as to be natural causes of everything that we might touch in our actions. We have free will in a world at the same time generally governed by God. Thus, we are currently in a position to know quite well that we could easily destroy virtually all life on this planet within exquisitely interconnected local ecologies, and we could have done most of the damage before the lifetime of our grandchildren is over.

As a species, we have already gone an impressive distance toward this end, by virtue of economic processes that we ourselves have created. Even given some truly inspired molders of economic and political power, we human beings are already tending to reduce by early death billions of people for the sake of paring down our numbers to a manageable few among the diverse cultures of this world, a feat already achieved in advance by murderous actions toward indigenous peoples. In particular, Americans did this centuries ago to the natives whom new settlers found as they, many of them "good Christian folk," violently took possession of the land eventually dubbed the (democratic republic of the) United States of America.

Now, sin accompanies the lives of regenerate Christians, but in Schleiermacher's understanding, all humans are still to be held responsible for our actions and for not responding to God's activity. We have already brought most of our kind to unsustainable levels of poverty and attendant ills. To obtain energy by extracting fossil fuels and cutting down forests, we have let international corporations wreak havoc at breakneck speed over the past century. The perhaps unintended consequences bear the pallid, externalizing titles "global warming" and "climate change."

Because it is the current world's largest and most powerful economy and largest consumer of energy, many now publicly proclaim that it is incumbent on the people of the United States and its leaders to move toward a global economy based on renewable sources of energy. They have good reason to expect this role, even though other countries are also taking the lead. As the self-acclaimed "greatest country on earth," it does bear the resources and influence necessary to bring the overwhelming majority of nations together in pursuing the aim on behalf of all human beings. In 2016, it joined nearly two hundred nations in signing the Paris climate accord, though the next president backed out.

Unfortunately, the world's free and unregulated economy has produced a tall curve of relative prosperity and wealth for a few billionaires

and an upper 10 percent composed of the very rich and some others relatively well-to-do because of pension plans and investments. The global
effects of the United States' recent major recession have not yet ended.
Some are hurting enough to call what has happened since 2008 a depression. I am inclined to agree, having gone through the Great Depression
in Dust Bowl mid-America in the 1930s myself. Caused by unregulated
financiers, the present downturn has placed lower- and working-class
people who live and strive within globally advanced but middle-class
bourgeoisie-run economies under still greater stress. The middle class has
become seriously depleted. Most of the rest of humanity is living in mar-
ginally improved, downgraded economies, despite the new educational
opportunities, health provisions, and technologies created since the early
nineteenth century. The "population explosion" deplored by experts since
the mid-1960s has continued to spread, its sum total unabated in our species' rat race to a huge disparity of income, rights, and opportunities. Ethi-
cally, equality is a vague chimera even in America, where the lions do not
lie down peaceably with the goats and the lambs.

Fortunately, for present purposes, I can pass the reader on to insight-
ful, best-selling investigator Naomi Klein for further information on these
themes. Her marvelously detailed and systematic account of the situation
is quite accessible, in a brilliantly thought-out and written, amply anno-
tated 564-page report, *This Changes Everything: Capitalism vs. the Climate*
(2016). Capitalism, for her, does not have to be totally destroyed, but
its practices do have to be transformed. Her book has come along none
too soon.

SCHLEIERMACHER AND SUSTAINABILITY

Long-term sustainability would be a large part of any effective plan sup-
portable by Schleiermacher's theology. From about 1990 to 1997, John
Cobb contributed to an initial rise of interest in ecotheology and sustainability. Cobb's book *Sustainability* (1992; reissued 2007) reports "turning
point" experiences in 1969, stimulated by Paul Ehrlich and Lynn White Jr.,
that put him on an "environmental" trajectory. In effect, this has been a
major focus of his vocation as a Christian leader and theologian to the very
present. This book is still of profound current value and strays very little
from Schleiermacher's principles, even though Cobb continually updates
his thinking by keeping up with pertinent sciences. It is rooted especially in the allied scientific outlook of the great English mathematician-
philosopher Alfred North Whitehead.[9]

Naomi Klein's complex presentation *This Changes Everything* is largely
consistent with Schleiermacher's philosophical worldview as well, even

its borrowing from theological language in offering a set of practices that serve to "regenerate" the present baleful ideological economics of early capitalist theory by an alternate economic worldview shriven of the old capitalism's ideological excesses, which have come to be dominant over the last century or so. Her heading for a section on how a sustainable shift to a "new economy" can happen is already beginning to occur: "Love Will Save This Place: Democracy, Divestment, and the Wins So Far."[10] What she notes in that section betokens the companionate, mutually benevolent love that Schleiermacher's theology features. It actually echoes his description of how God operates. While holding up Naomi Klein's masterpiece, which presents the same claim, it is necessary to backtrack a bit, to fill in what she and we have come to see.

The divides that have held us up in facing deep sins and errors in our American culture for a hundred years are distinctly ideological. In 1970, at nearly forty years of age, I wrote a second dissertation, this time in philosophy, at the University of Michigan. Titled "Ideology Old and New," it was a historical and comparative philosophical analysis of that term with an aim of providing a clarified and psychologically more accurate definition for use in social discourse.[11] I still find that, most simply defined, "ideology" points to (1) a set of values held within, (2) consciously or unconsciously expressed in various ways as to priority or degree, (3) in relation to a given social domain. When those sets of values tend to cohere or to agree in substance, an ideology becomes a worldview (*Weltanschauung*)—rare or popular, good or bad, powerful or a matter of indifference. Schleiermacher, via Wilhelm Dilthey's appropriation, is the originator of this larger concept. I also find that the worldview he purveyed joins other worldviews that influenced me even before I discovered their having drawn directly from Schleiermacher's influence.

A recital of some of these influences can illustrate how one's awareness of phenomena related to climate change can develop and, at the same time, how denials of how these phenomena have also been formed by so many.[12] Among my first influences on the subject of ideological substructures of one's self was Frank Buchman's Oxford Movement in China before World War II, which during that war had become Moral Re-Armament (MRA). In the 1950s, this movement went on the road as musical theater, Up with People.[13] MRA's "ideology of inspired democracy" bore a strong influence on me as a budding theologian wedded to the thought of Martin Buber, who, I learned much later, had drawn key elements of his own dialogical and inclusively egalitarian outlook directly from reading Schleiermacher.

This pattern also came to be the case in the lives of other scholars who had preceded the time when I was becoming a Schleiermacher expert in the 1960s. Most notable among them is John Dewey, whose pointedly nonreligious oeuvre I began to study, having discovered as a sophomore his masterful *Reconstruction in Philosophy* (1920). Dewey's book was among the early paperbacks published in America (reissued in paper, 1950). Much later I used others of his works in teaching courses in philosophy and in social foundations of education over nearly thirty years at Michigan without coming across a single direct clue regarding Schleiermacher's influence. Dewey himself had left almost no direct or self-acknowledged traces.[14] Although Schleiermacher was unmistakably a pragmatist and an evangelical liberal, wholly oriented to the gospel of Christ, he continues to influence people across a broad spectrum of beliefs and practices, especially theologians. Sometimes this influence occurred oddly or mistakenly, despite the unusual, constant care he took to make the results of studies issuing from his own extraordinary genius clear, no doubt in part because of the openness and inclusiveness of Schleiermacher's organum of studies.[15] Dewey too would be able to detect exactly what to do about reversing climate change today and replacing patterns of behavior from the money culture and individualism that have brought us to this crisis. He would replace these habits with communal and truly democratic ones.[16]

Following his decades of thoroughgoing research, I would endorse economist Robert Pollin's general strategy for reducing current global greenhouse gas levels by at least 40 percent in the next twenty years or less, then another 40 to 60 percent by 2065. The strategy would shift employment from jobs extracting and providing fossil fuels to the jobs necessary to obtain and sustain reliance on clean, renewable sources of energy. What is largely missing among the factors that Pollin and his colleagues report in the most recent of his works,[17] however, are the religious and moral, socially interactive principles and corresponding patterns of action required to create a new economy that Schleiermacher's worldview would advance, as would Klein's.

Experts like Pollin have led me to believe that our species can do even better than to reach the modest goals that he proposes, if we learn how to live out these principles and to join hands for the purpose. Already divestment tactics have had a strong effect on the markets for fossil fuels (coal, oil, natural gas). The industries have also begun to downsize, releasing personnel into fast-growing markets for relatively clean renewables, especially from wind and solar, geothermal, and small-scale hydro-generated resources. In addition to expanding grids for storing and transmitting electrical energy, the previous US administration (Barack Obama's) was raising standards for fuel consumption, requiring cleaner power plants, and reducing the greatly more damaging methane emissions. Donald Trump's administration is undoing such efforts. A significantly powerful ingredient also resides within the spiritual force for good that God in Christ has already bestowed upon Christian churches here on the North

American continent and among our sisters and brothers elsewhere, working together around the globe.[18]

As citizens we can push our governments and stimulate businesses to invest more than the 1.5–2 percent average global gross domestic product (GDP) per year that Pollin recommends, to achieve more than the 80 percent drop that he focuses on achieving in CO_2 emissions by 2050, which is more ambitious than the Paris accord's goal, set in 2016. We can also require, as Pollin would, investments in conservation and energy efficiency. Whereas China and the United States have been consuming about 39 percent of the world's energy and producing 42 percent of CO_2 emissions, the United States' consumption rate per capita is about four times higher than China's and its CO_2 rate is nearly three times higher. Pollin assumes an annual reduction from the current annual CO_2 emissions at 2.2 tons per capita each year, a reduction from a recent level of 16.7 tons per capita. We can do better than that, as increasing numbers are already doing, starting with a rapid reduction in our household carbon footprints and moving to concerted efforts at reduction by means that few citizens can control by themselves.

THE NITTY-GRITTY URGENCY OF DOING SOMETHING

According to Schleiermacher, under God and in Christ, the Christian church is called to influence the world. What else can Christians do, with other children of God, to reverse climate change?[19] Right off, we can ask for forgiveness in view of the sin we now commit every day as contributors to climate change. Sin is whatever gets in the way of one's growing relationship with God, in partnership with what one might have come to feel and perceive in Jesus, who is taken by many to be their Redeemer, even the Christ of all. Evil is a by-product of sin. Schleiermacher preached: "The direction [of our striving] must go against sin, not against evil." Yet as the church has oft declared, "a continuation of evil cannot be desired when it is viewed as a hindrance to life." This is especially so, he explains, because it is a hindrance to our consciousness of God.[20] His view easily leads to the cry: Dig up that root! Sin can be shared, but it starts within. Divine grace and our own gracious actions do, too. Schleiermacher was a liberal-leaning, gospel-oriented thinker, in that he was a firm and active believer in issuing forces for social justice, freedom, equal rights and treatment, and compassion. His life with God in Christ led him also to believe that these are principles of concrete behavior that love requires.

Accordingly, we can educate ourselves enough to know how we can reduce our own carbon footprint.[21] After former vice president Al Gore woke up our nation to the threats of climate change with the 2006 film

An Inconvenient Truth, he founded and continues to lead an organization called Climate Reality Project, which now has over 3.5 million members, including a great many young people.[22] The project conducts leadership training worldwide, and especially in the United States. To put the matter more directly: each of us can acknowledge that we are part of the problem, but each must also become part of the solution. We can easily take action right where we live, in our own households, every day. We can reinvest in renewables (primarily wind and solar), and in many instances, our electric bills can also be paid in this way.

By using the resources mentioned in this chapter, we can join others in making a larger impact, as we are able, toward completely reversing climate change within twenty years. People in most other countries will be doing these things, too. So will people in this country who belong to no church. Join their company. Think globally, act locally![23] This is a world-changing, dynamic program. It must include every human being possible and treat every human being as the best of us would do, living up to what we were created for. I conclude, therefore, with pleas to those who have been intrigued by or convinced of the power of Schleiermacher's theology and its potential for ecological living.

Do not fall for the climate of fear that dictators around the world seek to foster. Slavery is its product. Do not let yourself succumb to the climate of racism and hate, which only leads to exclusion and violence. Instead, join fully into the human race with those who would help the poor and down-trodden, the degraded and oppressed, rise to lives of dignity and integrity. Seek to satisfy your understandable need for security by enabling a better life for everyone. That is the gospel to which Schleiermacher led his university students of theology and his own congregation. It is what he would encourage you to share in your own life today. It is also the only way you, as a Christian, can confidently put your oar to the water to bring about an end to global warming while turning the harsher competitive tools of capitalism into the more salubrious cooperative tools—which can belong to both capitalism and the aims of solidarity, imperative tools that have long brought owners and workers to the same table.

The justice, freedom, equality, compassion, and love that marked practical results in Schleiermacher's own theological outlook can become yours to meet as well. True, there is no royal road to perfection, except in the world that dreams are made of. But it is also true both that there is safety in numbers, in masses of people striving together, and that we do not always get a fair shake while the world is being remade. Find the calm acceptance and gratitude within that Schleiermacher did, and share the joy that he did, of accomplishing what is good and right with people within the church, if you be so lucky (for in the church we are all sinners, too, though beloved sinners as we continue to grow there). In any case, accomplish what is good outside it if we will or must, for the visible church, like the rest of the world, can sometimes be very disappointing—slow to move, poor, nasty, and even brutish and short-lived. Schleiermacher encourages us to hitch a ride with the invisible church of God's Spirit in Christ, while growing to love the very real, visible, and ever-renewing church as well.

Beyond these things, you'll have to explore what attracts you most to do, always starting locally, where you can be in ready reach of others with whom to share an important, exciting part of your life. You'll be curious to learn more about how ecologically structured the earth is, for it is your environment. Perhaps some of what you choose to do will enjoy global reach. If it serves to change what energy is used, how it is used locally, by whom and for what and for whom, it surely will belong to the general ecological whole that is earth and that both exists now and is coming into being in fresh new forms.

NOTES

INTRODUCTION

1. For a helpful introduction to Schleiermacher's life and work, see Theodore Vial, *Schleiermacher: A Guide for the Perplexed* (London: Bloomsbury T&T Clark, 2013); see also Brian A. Gerrish, *A Prince of the Church: Schleiermacher and the Beginnings of Modern Theology* (Eugene, OR: Wipf & Stock, 2001); Terrence N. Tice, *Schleiermacher* (Nashville: Abingdon Press, 2006).

2. For a summary of the broad interpretive view of the history of modern theology made popular by Karl Barth's followers, see Van A. Harvey, "A Word in Defense of Schleiermacher's Theological Method," *Journal of Religion* 42, no. 3 (1962): 151–70. See also Emil Brunner's early critique of Schleiermacher in *Die Mystik und Das Wort: Der Gegensatz zwischen moderner Religionsauffassung und christlichem Glauben* (Tübingen: J. C. B. Mohr, 1924); Hugh Ross Mackintosh, *Types of Modern Theology: Schleiermacher to Barth* (London: Nisbet and Co., 1937); and George Lindbeck, *The Nature of Doctrine: Religion and Theology in a Postliberal Age* (Louisville, KY: Westminster/John Knox Press, 1984).

3. See Brian A. Gerrish, *Continuing the Reformation: Essays on Modern Religious Thought* (Chicago: University of Chicago Press, 1993); Dawn DeVries, *Jesus Christ in the Preaching of Calvin and Schleiermacher* (Louisville, KY: Westminster John Knox Press, 1996); Catherine L. Kelsey, *Thinking about Christ with Schleiermacher* (Louisville, KY: Westminster John Knox Press, 2003); Kevin Hector, *Theology without Metaphysics: God, Language, and the Spirit of Recognition* (New York: Cambridge University Press, 2011); idem, "Actualism and Incarnation: The High Christology of Friedrich Schleiermacher," *International Journal of Systematic Theology* 8, no. 3 (July 2006): 307–22; Christine Helmer, *Theology and the End of Doctrine* (Louisville, KY: Westminster John Knox Press, 2014); Paul Nimmo, "Schleiermacher on Scripture and the Work of Jesus Christ," *Modern Theology* 31, no. 1 (January 2015): 60–90; idem, "Schleiermacher on Justification: A Departure from the Reformation?," *Scottish Journal of Theology* 66, no. 1 (2013): 50–73; Brent W. Sockness and Wilhelm Gräb, eds., *Schleiermacher, the Study of Religion, and the Future of Theology: A Transatlantic Dialogue* (New York: Walter de Gruyter, 2010).

4. *Naturzusammenhang* has been translated as "interconnected process of nature" in Friedrich Schleiermacher, *Christian Faith: A New Translation and Critical Edition*, trans. Terrence N. Tice, Catherine L. Kelsey, and Edwina Lawler, ed. Catherine L. Kelsey and Terrence N. Tice, 2 vols. (Louisville, KY: Westminster John Knox Press, 2016). Hereafter cited as *CF*.

1. SCHLEIERMACHER ON CHURCH AND CHRISTIAN ETHICS

1. Immanuel Kant, *The Critique of Practical Reason*, trans. Lewis White Beck (Indianapolis: Bobbs-Merrill Educational Publishing, 1956).

2. Claude Welch, *Protestant Thought in the Nineteenth Century*, 2 vols. (New Haven, CT: Yale University Press, 1985), 1:47.

3. In this regard see Kevin W. Hector, *Theology without Metaphysics: God, Language, and the Spirit of Recognition* (New York: Cambridge University Press, 2011). Hector engages Schleiermacher in developing his own argument that language cannot capture the essence of an object or represent the structure of an object exhaustively. He argues that truthful speech intends to continue a practice, recognizes the authority of precedents, and attempts to produce a recognizable continuation of what the precedents are about. Hector's project has clear affinities to Schleiermacher's turn to feeling and to a community grounded in tradition, and his revisionist appropriation and continuation of that tradition.

4. Representative rationalist theologians include Julius Wegschneider and Johann Roehr; significant supernaturalists include Gottlieb Christian Storr and Claus Harms. For a fine overview of the development and conflict between these two schools, see Kevin M. Vander Schel, *Embedded Grace: Christ, History, and the Reign of God in Schleiermacher's Dogmatics* (Minneapolis: Fortress Press, 2013), 1–38.

5. See the discussion of providence in chap. 4 below for an example of the way that Schleiermacher transcends naturalism and supernaturalism in his thinking about divine and natural causation. Chap. 4 identifies the dynamic relation between providence and the interconnected process of nature that holds together free events in the world and God's providential purpose for the world. Human agency and God's providence come together in a teleological drive toward the reign of God and the wholeness of all creation.

6. B. A. Gerrish, *Tradition and the Modern World* (Chicago: University of Chicago Press, 1978), 40. See also 52 and 68–69, where Gerrish indicates how Schleiermacher transcends and synthesizes the Protestant orthodox and sectarian views of the church.

7. Karl Barth, *The Theology of Schleiermacher*, ed. Dietrich Ritschl, trans. Geoffrey W. Bromiley (Grand Rapids: Wm. B. Eerdmans Publishing Co., 1982), 278.

8. See the call to action that concludes this volume. The call to educate ourselves about our ecological plight, to reduce our carbon footprint, to resist the climate of fear, and to live in ecologically sustainable ways—responding to the signal social-ethical challenge of our day—has clear parallels to the specific actions that Schleiermacher took in his own context to further concrete reform of society and church.

9. Robert M. Bigler, *The Politics of German Protestantism: The Rise of the Protestant Church Elite in Prussia, 1815–1848* (Berkeley: University of California Press, 1972), 32.

10. *Selections from Friedrich Schleiermacher's* Christian Ethics, ed. and trans. James M. Brandt (Louisville, KY: Westminster John Knox Press, 2011), 23. Hereafter citations of this translation are abbreviated as *CE*. The standard edition of Schleiermacher's *Christliche Sittenlehre* or *Christian Ethics* has been *Die christliche Sitte nach den Grundsätzen der evangelischen Kirche im Zusammenhange dargestellt*, ed. Ludwig Jonas, *Sämmtliche Werke* I.12 (Berlin: G. Reimer, 1843), hereafter referred to as *Sittenlehre*. Translations of it in this work are the authors' own. In 2010 Hermann

Peiter published a version of the *Christliche Sittenlehre* based on the 1826–27 lectures: F. D. E. Schleiermacher, *Christliche Sittenlehre (Vorlesung im Wintersemester 1826/27). Nach grössenteils unveröffentlichten Hörernachschriften und nach teilweise unveröffentlichten Manuskripten Schleiermachers*, ed. Hermann Peiter (Berlin: LIT Verlag, 2010).

11. In his introduction to the reprint edition of the *Christliche Sittenlehre*, Wolfgang Erich Mueller notes that the descriptive approach corresponds to the need to reflect on the current cultural situation. A biblical ethics or an imperative ethics would not meet this requirement. Wolfgang Erich Mueller, introduction to *Die christliche Sitte nach den Grundsätzen der evangelischen Kirche im Zusammenhang dargestellt*, by Friedrich Schleiermacher, Theologische Studien-Texte 7.1 (Waltrop: Spenner, 1999), xviii.

12. Friedrich Schleiermacher, *Der christliche Glaube nach den Grundsätzen der evangelischen Kirche im Zusammenhange dargestellt (1830–31)*, ed. Rolf Schäfer (Berlin: Walter de Gruyter, 2003), *KGA* I.13. Hereafter referred to as *CG*. Translations are my own except where cited from the recent English translation, *Christian Faith* (abbreviated *CF*). See *CG* §§113–63, pp. 229–493, for the analysis of the church; §§157–63, pp. 456–93, for "The Perfection of the Church."

13. For considerations of Schleiermacher's eschatology, see Eilert Herms, "Schleiermachers Eschatologie," *Theologische Zeitschrift* 46 (1990): 97–123; Martin Weeber, *Schleiermachers Eschatologie: Eine Untersuchung zum theologischen Spätwerk* (Gütersloh: Christian Kaiser, 2000); Bernd Oberdorfer, "Schleiermacher on Eschatology and Resurrection," in *Resurrection: Theological and Scientific Assessments*, ed. Ted Peters, Robert J. Russell, and Michael Welker (Grand Rapids: Wm. B. Eerdmans Publishing Co., 2002), 165–82.

14. *CG* §158.2, p. 461.

15. This topic is taken up again in the next chapter of this volume.

16. *CG* postscript to §163, p. 492.

17. *CG* §157.1, p. 456.

18. *CG* §157.2, p. 457.

19. Ibid.

20. *CG* §157.2, p. 458.

21. *CG* §157, p. 456.

22. See chap. 2 below for an assessment of Schleiermacher's eschatological thought that points out the way he allows for thought of an afterlife primarily as a way to deal with the dissonance resulting from the traditional concept of reprobation. The analysis of chap. 2 provides a helpful complement to the argument here that eschatology is rendered significant by its ethical purchase.

23. *CG* §§9.1, 9.2; pp. 77, 79.

24. *CG* §56.2, pp. 355–56.

25. *CE* 25.

26. *CE* 108.

27. For an important exposition of Schleiermacher that lifts up his sense of embodied self-consciousness, see Thandeka, *The Embodied Self: Friedrich Schleiermacher's Solution to Kant's Problem of the Empirical Self* (Albany: State University of New York Press, 1995), 25.

28. Eilert Herms, "Reich Gottes und menschliches Handeln," in *Friedrich Schleiermacher 1768–1834: Theologe, Philosoph, Pädagoge*, ed. Dietz Lange (Göttingen: Vandenhoeck & Ruprecht, 1985), 187.

29. Not least Emil Brunner. See Brunner, *The Divine Imperative*, trans. Olive Wyon (Philadelphia: Westminster Press, 1947). He speaks of Schleiermacher's ethics as "psychologically subjective" (573).

30. Gerrish, *Tradition and the Modern World*, 41. That Schleiermacher's theology can be understood as a "sociology of religious consciousness" is not to say that his theology can be reduced to sociology, only that the social character of his *theological* program is undeniable.

31. *CF* §87, p. 544.

32. *CF* §87.3, p. 546.

33. *CF* §93.1, p. 565.

34. *CF* §100.2, p. 625.

35. *CF* §117.1, p. 767.

36. However, because of Schleiermacher's questioning of immortality as central to the life of faith, there is room here for development of his thought. Chap. 2 will return to this idea.

37. *CF* §116.3, p. 765.

38. See *CF* §117.1, p. 767.

39. *CF* §121.2, p. 799.

40. *Sittenlehre*, 122.

41. Roger Haight, SJ, *Christian Community in History*, vol. 3, *Ecclesial Existence* (New York: Continuum, 2008), 51.

42. Ibid., 52.

43. Again, the next chapter of this volume will return to this important theme.

44. See the introduction to this book and its discussion of how the inner/ outer distinction is taken up and employed to structure the movement of this volume. For Schleiermacher, the inner/outer distinction and related church/world distinction are not rigid separations, but two poles at the opposite ends of a continuum and polar opposites that inhabit each other. So the church is in the world and the world exists within the church. For Schleiermacher, movement in both life and thought occurs as there is oscillation between polar opposites. The authors hope that such movement obtains within and among the chapters of this volume.

45. Vander Schel, *Embedded Grace*, 195–96 n. 59.

46. Haight, *Ecclesial Existence*, 64.

47. Christopher Evans, *Liberalism without Illusions: Renewing an American Christian Tradition* (Waco, TX: Baylor University Press, 2010).

48. Ibid., 148.

49. *CE* 31.

50. Ibid.

51. This is clearly an allusion to Schleiermacher's contemporary Friedrich Ludwig Jahn, the father of German gymnastics. Jahn advocated physical exercise as a way to attain fitness and health.

52. Examples of statements by Protestant churches in the United States that call for reform related to the ecological situation include Susan Evans and Mary Minette, "Hunger and Climate Change: Agriculture and Food Security in a Changing Climate," a 2010 document of the Evangelical Lutheran Church in America that identifies ways in which issues of hunger and climate change are deeply interconnected and names ways individuals and congregations can increase awareness and act responsibly (goo.gl/aqnuLg); "The Power to Change: U.S. Energy Policy

and Global Warming," a statement approved by the 218th General Assembly of the Presbyterian Church (U.S.A.), which lays out the theological rationale for addressing ecological challenges and recommendations for action by individuals, congregations, and judicatories (https://www.presbyterianmission.org); a 2016 video from the Episcopal Church, "Environmental Issues and the Anglican Communion," which presents the crucial ecological issues facing the world and the call for Christians to join in responding to these issues (https://www.episcopal church.org/library/video/environmental-issues-and-anglican-communion); and "United Church of Christ Report on Environmental Racism" (2017), which outlines the way communities of color are intentionally targeted as locations for hazardous waste sites, landfills, and polluting industries and provides suggestions for advocacy in relation to environmental racism (http://www.ucc.org).

53. See *Sittenlehre*, 300–304.

54. *Sittenlehre*, 322.

55. *CE* 107. See chap. 5 below for further analysis of the importance of formation of individuals and communities as part of the inner mission of the church. A crucial goal of this formation is to build capacity to care for and cultivate the natural world in a discerning way.

56. *Sittenlehre*, 310.

57. *Sittenlehre*, 384–85.

58. *CE* 144. See 143–46 for the discussion of the relation between presentational action and community. *Sittenlehre*, 509–14.

59. *CE* 144.

60. *CE* 151.

61. The German word that signifies public worship, *Gottesdienst*, literally means "service of God." The German term expresses well the dual sense of worship for Schleiermacher, including both formal, liturgical worship and the broader sense of service to God in daily life.

62. *Sittenlehre*, 265–66.

63. Hans-Joachim Birkner, *Schleiermachers christliche Sittenlehre im Zusammenhang seines philosophisch-theologischen Systems*, Theologische Bibliothek Töpelmann (Berlin: Alfred Töpelmann, 1964), 96–97.

64. On the "principle of openness," see *Sittenlehre*, 189, 216, 272.

65. *CE* 167–73.

66. *CE* 173. Schleiermacher identifies purity, patience, forbearance, and humility as the Christian virtues. See *Sittenlehre*, 607–16.

67. *Sittenlehre*, 641–42.

2. AN ECOLOGICAL *OIKOS*

1. A version of this chapter was first published as Shelli M. Poe, "Friedrich Schleiermacher's Theology as a Resource for Ecological Economics," *Theology Today* 73, no. 1 (2016): 9–23. A portion also appears in the concluding chapter of Shelli M. Poe, *Essential Trinitarianism: Schleiermacher as Trinitarian Theologian*, T&T Clark Explorations in Reformed Theology (New York: Bloomsbury, 2017). The material was originally delivered to the Schleiermacher Group of the American

Academy of Religion in 2014. I am indebted to the active members of the Schleiermacher Group for their feedback on the original paper.

2. Sallie McFague, "God's Household: Christianity, Economics, and Planetary Living," in *Subverting Greed: Religious Perspectives in the Global Economy*, ed. Paul F. Knitter and Chandra Muzaffar (Maryknoll, NY: Orbis Books, 2002), 120.

3. By making this suggestion, I follow Schleiermacher's own understanding of the close relationship between theology and Christian ethics. Cf. *CF* §169.3, p. 1017; Schleiermacher, *On Religion: Speeches to Its Cultured Despisers*, trans. and ed. Richard Crouter (New York: Cambridge University Press, 1996), 118–19.

4. Chap. 5 presents Schleiermacher's doctrine of election in further detail.

5. *CF* §119.3, p. 783.

6. McFague, "God's Household," 124.

7. Ibid., 126. See also Rosemary Radford Ruether, *Integrating Ecofeminism, Globalization, and World Religions* (New York: Rowman & Littlefield, 2005), 33–36.

8. McFague, "God's Household," 125–26.

9. Ibid., 124.

10. Ruether, *Integrating Ecofeminism*, 79.

11. McFague, "God's Household," 128. In another context, Kathryn Tanner describes such free services as benefits properly bestowed on all people, "whether or not you can pay for them or have done the giver a good turn, even if you've misused them, and so forth." Kathryn Tanner, *Economy of Grace* (Minneapolis: Fortress Press, 2005), 62.

12. McFague, "God's Household," 126. Cf. Tanner, *Economy of Grace*, 74.

13. As his *Christian Faith* is the work in which Schleiermacher's mature theology appears, I have prioritized its analysis. However, further connections may be made to show the coherence of Schleiermacher's epistemology, ontology, theory of religion, and theology with regard to the *Naturzusammenhang*. For a brief analysis, see Terrence Tice's introduction to Schleiermacher's *Dialectic; or, The Art of Doing Philosophy* (Atlanta: Scholars Press, 1996), xix–xxv. Footnotes throughout the chapter relating portions of *Christian Faith* to *On Religion* and *Dialectic* point the reader toward a fuller account of the *Naturzusammenhang* in Schleiermacher's corpus.

14. *CF* §38.2, p. 214. See also Friedrich Schleiermacher, *On the Doctrine of Election, with Special Reference to the Aphorisms of Dr. Bretschneider*, Columbia Series in Reformed Theology, trans. Iain G. Nicol and Allen G. Jorgenson (Louisville, KY: Westminster John Knox Press, 2006); and Matthias Gockel, *Barth and Schleiermacher on the Doctrine of Election: A Systematic-Theological Comparison* (New York: Oxford University Press, 2006), 37–103. In the *Dialectic*, the unity of thinking and being is maintained to avoid an original duality; see *Dialectic*, 41–42.

15. *CF* §46.1, p. 248. Schleiermacher is also able to make claims like the following: "We are involved in forming a vital perspective on the deity to the extent that we work on the completion of the real sciences. This happens, however, not when a detail is added to other details merely as an aggregate but only through systematic treatment in which the totality of all this is at least striven for" (*Dialectic*, 38). Here he emphasizes the oneness of knowledge that corresponds to the unity of the *Naturzusammenhang*.

16. *CF* §58.2, p. 344. Cf. Andrew Dole, *Schleiermacher on Religion and the Natural Order* (New York: Oxford University Press, 2010). The interconnectivity of the whole is also found in Schleiermacher's epistemology. See Schleiermacher, *Dialectic*, 7, 16–17.

17. As such, Schleiermacher's work takes account of the emerging modern scientific view of the natural world by avoiding any sense of divine intervention within the interconnected process of nature. Chap. 3 expands on the noninterventionist stance Schleiermacher takes here.

18. See Schleiermacher, *Dialectic*, 31, 39. See also Jon Paul Sydnor, *Ramanuja and Schleiermacher: Toward a Constructive Comparative Theology* (Cambridge: James Clarke & Co., 2012), 145–46.

19. *CF* §46.2, p. 252.

20. *CF* §46, p. 248.

21. Schleiermacher, *Dialectic*, 43. Cf. *CF* §58.1, p. 343.

22. *CF* §72.3, p. 440.

23. *CF* §72.3, p. 441. Compare with Judith Butler's understanding of the constitution of universal concepts. She describes that formation as an open-ended process of constitution and reconstitution that leaves room for "unknowingness about what [the universal] is and what it might include in a future not fully determined in advance." Judith Butler, *Undoing Gender* (New York: Routledge, 2004), 191.

24. *CF* §60.2, p. 360. Cf. Schleiermacher, *Dialectic*, 57.

25. *CF* §120.3, p. 790.

26. *CF* §97.4, pp. 605–6.

27. For an introduction to Schleiermacher's Christology, see Kevin Hector, "Actualism and Incarnation: The High Christology of Friedrich Schleiermacher," *International Journal of Systematic Theology* 8, no. 3 (July 2006): 307–22.

28. *CF* §97.2, p. 595.

29. For analyses of Schleiermacher's doctrine of election, see Gockel, *Barth and Schleiermacher*; Anette I. Hagan, *Eternal Blessedness for All? A Historical-Systematic Examination of Friedrich Schleiermacher's Reinterpretation of Predestination* (Eugene, OR: Pickwick Publications, 2013); Sung-Sup Kim, *Deus Providebit: Calvin, Schleiermacher, and Barth on the Providence of God*, Emerging Scholars Series (Minneapolis: Fortress Press, 2014).

30. *CF* §119.2, p. 782.

31. *CF* §120.2, pp. 788–89.

32. *CF* §120.2, p. 789.

33. *CF* §120.4, p. 793.

34. Schleiermacher attempts to balance the individual with the *Naturzusammenhang*, as in *Dialectic*, 72: "If one throws everything into the class of life in general, one kills what is individual and subjects are then mere points of transition, operating mechanistically. If one throws everything into the class of individual life, one kills the interconnectedness, operating magically."

35. *CF* §120.4, p. 793.

36. *CF* §120.3, pp. 790–91.

37. Sarah Coakley, *Christ without Absolutes* (New York: Clarendon Press, 1995), 143 n. See also *CF* §164.1, p. 999; and Schleiermacher, *Dialectic*, 7.

38. We will return to the corporate nature of sin and redemption in chap. 5.

39. *CF* §118–118.1, pp. 771–72.

40. *CF* §118.1, p. 772.

41. *CF* §119.3, p. 783.

42. *CF* §118.1, p. 772.

43. *CF* §158.3, p. 973.

44. *CF* §158.2, p. 970.

45. *CF* §159.2, p. 976.

46. *CF* §158.2, p. 970.

47. *CF* §158.1, p. 968.

48. *CF* §158.1, p. 967.

49. See chap. 1 for another analysis of the character and importance of eschatological themes in Schleiermacher's theology. Chap. 1 argues, in a manner quite consistent with the argument in this chapter, that, while Schleiermacher does not reject the notion of personal survival after death out of hand, the focus of his eschatological thinking is on the reign of God as a call to action in the present.

50. *CF* §158.2, p. 970.

51. *CF* §118.2, p. 777.

52. Schleiermacher explains, "Every element of doctrine that is constructed in the spirit of a desire to hold fast that which is already a matter of general acknowledgement, along with the natural inferences therefrom, is of an orthodox character; every element constructed with a tendency to keep the System of Doctrine in a state of mobility, and to make room for other modes of apprehension, is heterodox." Friedrich Schleiermacher, *Brief Outline of the Study of Theology*, trans. William Farrer (1850; repr. Eugene, OR: Wipf & Stock, 2007), 165. Schleiermacher made many heterodox suggestions in his mature work. As he says, "I am firmly convinced, however, that my position is an inspired heterodoxy that in due time will become orthodox, although certainly not just because of my book and perhaps not until long after my death." Friedrich Schleiermacher, *On the* Glaubenslehre: *Two Letters to Dr. Lücke*, trans. James Duke and Francis Fiorenza (Atlanta: Scholars Press, 1981), 53. For more on heterodoxy, see Thomas H. Curran, *Doctrine and Speculation in Schleiermacher's Glaubenslehre* (New York: Walter de Gruyter, 1994), 285–95.

53. See Daniel Pedersen, "Eternal Life in Schleiermacher's *The Christian Faith*," *International Journal of Systematic Theology* 13, no. 3 (July 2011): 340–57. I wish to thank Daniel Pedersen for our extended personal correspondence on this topic. Though we remain in disagreement over the significance of immortality in Schleiermacher's theology, we have found many more similarities than differences in our overall interpretations of Schleiermacher's work.

54. Ibid., 341.

55. See also Nathan D. Hieb, "The Precarious State of Resurrection in Friedrich Schleiermacher's *Glaubenslehre*," *International Journal of Systematic Theology* 9, no. 4 (2007): 398–414; and Abraham Varghese Kunnuthara, *Schleiermacher on Christian Consciousness of God's Work in History*, Princeton Theological Monograph Series 76 (Eugene, OR: Pickwick Publications, 2008).

56. *CF* postscript to §120, p. 796.

57. Cf. Schleiermacher, *On Religion*, 112: "the whole development of this religion in all generations and individuals is just as historically tied to this moment."

58. *CF* §160.1, p. 979.

59. *CF* §160.2, p. 980.

60. *CF* §163.1, p. 992.

61. *CF* §120.4, p. 793. See also Schleiermacher, *On Religion*, 116: "All evil, even that which the finite must commit before it has completely run the course of its existence, is a consequence of the will, of the self-seeking endeavor of individual nature that everywhere tears itself loose from the relationship with the whole in order to be something for itself."

62. Sallie McFague, *Life Abundant: Rethinking Theology and Economy for a Planet in Peril* (Minneapolis: Fortress Press, 2001), 77.

63. See Joerg Rieger, *Christ and Empire* (Minneapolis: Fortress Press, 2007).

64. I am using "ecumenical" here in a broad sense to include both intra- and interreligious dialogue. Although this is not the standard usage of the term, it helpfully retains the etymological link between ecology, economics, and ecumenism, noted above.

65. *CF* §72.4, p. 447. See also *CF* §100.2, p. 625.

66. *CF* §117.1, p. 767.

67. *CF* §157.2, p. 966.

68. *CF* §157.2, p. 967.

69. *CF* §157.1, p. 966.

70. *CF* §157, p. 965.

71. *CF* §157, p. 965.

72. *CF* §157.2, p. 967.

73. *CF* postscript to §163, p. 998.

74. *CF* §160.2, p. 980.

75. *CF* §162.1, p. 988.

76. *CF* postscript to §163, p. 998.

77. *CF* §2.1, p. 4.

78. *CF* §11, p. 79. Cf. Schleiermacher, *On Religion*, 112.

79. *CF* §119.2, pp. 782, 781.

80. *CF* §117, p. 767.

81. Schleiermacher makes these regrettable statements in other portions of his corpus as well. See, for instance, *On Religion*, 113–14, 116.

82. *CF* §12.1, p. 90.

83. *CF* §93.4, p. 573. Cf. Schleiermacher, *On Religion*, 108.

84. For instance, Schleiermacher recognizes that Jesus adopted the notion of the resurrection of the dead "that was prevalent among his people." See *CF* §161, p. 981.

85. Schleiermacher, *On Religion*, 109–11, 114.

86. Thomas Reynolds, "Reconsidering Schleiermacher and the Problem of Religious Diversity," *Journal of the American Academy of Religion* 73, no. 1 (March 2005): 171, 172.

87. *CF* §120.3, p. 792.

88. Schleiermacher, *On Religion*, 123.

89. Schleiermacher, *On Religion*, 97–98, 104.

90. *CF* §164.1, pp. 999–1000.

91. *CF* postscript to §163, p. 998.

3. SCHLEIERMACHER'S THEOLOGICAL NATURALISM

1. "Schleiermacher to F. H. Jacobi. Berlin, March 30, 1818," in *Schleiermacher: Christian Dialogue, The Second Speech, and Other Selections*, edited, translated, and with an introduction by Julia A. Lamm (New York: Paulist Press, 2014), 262.

2. *CF* §54.4, p. 310. "For everything that happens temporally and spatially also has its conditions in the totality of what is outside it and before it, however

much these factors might be hidden from us thus far." See also §46.2, p. 253: "natural causation, viewed as the complete conditionality of all that happens through the general interconnected process of nature."

3. For a synopsis of consumption as a global ecological threat, and a brief description of some of the barriers to effecting the changes that we need, see Peter Dauvergne, "The Problem of Consumption," *Global Environmental Politics* 10, no. 2 (2010): 1–10. For an argument that the use of the term "sustainability" by businesses masks and encourages, rather than reduces, consumption, see Dauvergne, "The Sustainability Story: Exposing Truths, Half-Truths, and Illusions," in *New Earth Politics: Essays from the Anthropocene*, ed. Simon Nicholson and Sikina Jinnah (Cambridge, MA: MIT Press, 2016), 387–404.

4. As Kent E. Portney suggests, it may be more accurate to speak of "concepts of sustainability," to signal the range of meanings that are given to "sustainability." A 1987 report from the United Nations' World Commission on Environment and Development, commonly referred to as the report of the Bruntland Commission, produced a definition of "sustainable development" that has been widely influential: "development that meets the needs of the present without compromising the ability of future generations to meet their own needs." The report identifies three interrelated elements of sustainable development: environment, economy, and equity. For a helpful summary of the concepts of sustainability and a history of the term "sustainability," see Kent E. Portney, *Sustainability* (Cambridge, MA: MIT Press, 2015), 1–56. For another helpful, detailed exposition of the concepts and their history, see Thomas Pfister, Martin Schweighofer, and André Reichel, *Sustainability* (New York: Routledge, 2016), 1–25. For very concise introductions to the term "sustainability," see esp.: Julian Agyeman, "Sustainability," in *Keywords for Environmental Studies*, ed. Joni Adamson, William A. Gleason, and David N. Pellow (New York: New York University Press, 2016), 186–89; Peter Dauvergne, "Sustainability," in *Historical Dictionary of Environmentalism*, 2nd ed. (Lanham, MD: Rowman & Littlefield, 2016), 195.

5. Among other things, "preconceptual" and "immediate" both imply that—strictly speaking—this feeling of absolute dependence does not include any self-representation (and for that reason, no thinking *about* ourselves).

6. *CF* §4.3, p. 24.

7. For especially clear expressions of the premise that divine activity does not occur in time or space, see *CF* postscript to §53, p. 304: "we always do posit [divine causality] to be absolutely nontemporal and nonspatial" and *CF* postscript to §53, p. 305: "the causality that evokes the feeling of absolute dependence in us cannot be temporal and cannot be spatial." See also *CG* postscript to §53, p. 287: "Because we, however, do not admit [that there are] any individual and temporal divine acts" (translation mine). For two especially clear expressions of the corollary that divine activity is not subject to contrasts, see *CF* §147.2, p. 933, where Schleiermacher refers to "our own initial basic presupposition that there exists no relationship of reciprocity between the creature and the Creator," and *CF* §164.3, p. 1001, where Schleiermacher reminds readers that "there is no division or contrast in the divine causality anywhere."

8. For Schleiermacher's calling it a "canon," see, for example, *CF* §97.2, p. 594: "the first canon that God would have to remain strictly identical beyond all the means and measures of time."

9. *CF* §40, p. 217.

10. *CF* §39.1, p. 215. Accordingly, theologians should have a defensive, primary aim when crafting a doctrine of creation: prevent nontheological claims (from, e.g., other branches of scientific inquiry) from "slipping into it" (*CF* §39.2, p. 216). Theologians have a more constructive task in the doctrine of preservation: "fully to present that basic feeling [of absolute dependence] itself" (§39, p. 215).

11. *CF* §41, p. 221.

12. The theology of Martin Luther provides notable examples of these ways of telling a creation story. See Johannes Schwanke, "Martin Luther's Doctrine of Creation," in *Oxford Research Encyclopedias of Religion*, doi:10.1093/acrefore/9780199340378.013.329.

13. Many Christian doctrines of creation use this trope. For a particularly well-known and influential use of it in Trinitarian terms, see Karl Barth, *Church Dogmatics*, III/1, *The Doctrine of Creation*, trans. J. W. Edwards, O. Bussey, and H. Knight, ed. G. W. Bromiley and T. F. Torrance (London: T&T Clark International, 2004), esp. 42–94.

14. The theology of Karl Rahner provides a notable example of this story line. See Karl Rahner, *The Foundations of Christian Faith: An Introduction to the Idea of Christianity*, trans. William V. Dych (New York: Crossroad Publishing, 1982), 116–37; Karl Rahner, *The Trinity*, trans. Joseph Donceel (New York: Crossroad Publishing, 1997).

15. The theology of Martin Luther provides an example of this story line. See Schwanke, "Martin Luther's Doctrine of Creation."

16. Arguably, any Christian doctrine of creation that formally appropriates the act of creation to the Father provides an example. For influential contemporary examples of theologies that appropriate the act of creation to God as Mother, see Sallie McFague, *Models of God: Theology for an Ecological, Nuclear Age* (Minneapolis: Fortress Press, 1987), 109–15, and Elizabeth A. Johnson, *She Who Is: The Mystery of God in Feminist Theological Discourse*, 10th anniv. ed. (New York: Crossroad Publishing, 2002), 179–214.

17. For an ecotheological proposal that critically appropriates Schleiermacher's theology in concert with a householder trope, see the chapter from Shelli M. Poe in this volume. See also Ernst M. Conradie, *The Earth in God's Economy: Creation, Salvation and Consummation in Ecological Perspective* (Zurich: LIT Verlag, 2015), 221–46.

18. *CG* §97.2, p. 76: "das Menschenwerden Gottes im Bewußtsein und das Gebildetwerden der menschlichen Natur zur Persönlichkeit Christi." See *CF* §97.2, p. 596.

19. *CF* §94.2, p. 576; §96.3, p. 589.

20. *CF* §94.2, pp. 576, 578.

21. *CF* §97.2, p. 594.

22. The emphasis conveyed by italics here is Schleiermacher's. In the German text, Schleiermacher emphasizes the singularity of that point in space and that moment in time by capitalizing *einem* (one) (*CG* §97.2). Normally, that word would not be capitalized in German. Tice, Kelsey, and Lawler have rightly "translated" Schleiermacher's emphasis into English by italicizing rather than capitalizing the word "one." *CF* §97.2, pp. 594–95.

23. *CF* §100.2, p. 623.

24. *CF* §165.1, p. 1004.

25. *CF* §166.1, p. 1005.

26. *CF* §164.3, pp. 1002, 1001.

27. *CF* §166.1, p. 1005.

28. *CF* §166.1, p. 1005.

29. *CF* §166.1, p. 1005.

30. *CF* §165.1, p. 1004.

31. *CF* §164.2, p. 1001.

32. *CF* §164.3, p. 1001. Again, the emphasis conveyed by the italics here is Schleiermacher's. See n. 22, above.

33. For German-language scholarship about Schleiermacher's understanding of nature, see, e.g., Wilhelm Dilthey, *Gesammelte Schriften*, v. 14, bd. 2, *Schleiermachers System als Philosophie und Theologie* (Leipzig: Teubner, 1985); Herman Süskind, *Der Einfluss Schellings auf die Entwicklung von Schleiermachers System* (Tübingen: J. C. B. Mohr, 1909); Hans-Joachim Birkner, *Schleiermachers christliche Sittenlehre im Zusammenhang seines philosophisch-theologischen Systems*, Theologische Bibliothek Töpelmann (Berlin: Alfred Töpelmann, 1964), 30–64; and Ueli Hasler, *Beherrschte Natur: Die Anpassung der Theologie an die bürgerliche Naturauffassung im 19. Jahrhundert (Schleiermacher, Ritschl, Herrmann)* (Bern: Peter Lang, 1982), 61–172.

34. For a longer treatment of Schleiermacher's understanding of nature, with specific attention to its relation to Spinoza's philosophy, see Julia A. Lamm, *The Living God: Schleiermacher's Theological Appropriation of Spinoza* (University Park: Pennsylvania State University Press, 1996). For a short treatment that is focused on Schleiermacher's determinism, see chap. 1 of Andrew Dole, *Schleiermacher on Religion and the Natural Order* (New York: Oxford University Press, 2010), 35–70. For an analysis of how Schleiermacher relates natural and moral law, see George N. Boyd, "Schleiermacher's 'Über den Unterschied zwischen Naturgesetz und Sittengesetz,'" *Journal of Religious Ethics* 17, no. 2 (Fall 1989): 41–49.

35. Friedrich Schleiermacher, *On Religion: Speeches to Its Cultured Despisers*, trans. and ed. Richard Crouter (New York: Cambridge University Press, 1996), 5.

36. Kant posited an "attractive force," which he defined as "that moving force by which a matter can be the cause of the approach of others to it (or, what is the same, by which it resists the removal of others from it)," and a "repulsive force," which he defined as "that by which a matter can be the cause of others removing themselves from it (or, what is the same, by which it resists the approach of others to it)." He reduced all other moving forces to these two: "only these two kinds of forces can be thought, as forces to which all moving forces in material nature must be reduced." Immanuel Kant, *Metaphysical Foundations of Natural Science*, trans. and ed. Michael Friedman (Cambridge: Cambridge University Press, 2004), 35–36.

37. Schleiermacher, *On Religion*, 5.

38. *KGA* II.10.1, *Vorlesungen über die Dialektik*, ed. Andreas Arndt (Berlin: de Gruyter, 2002), 137.

39. Ibid.

40. Friedrich Schleiermacher, *Friedrich Schleiermachers sämmtliche Werke, Dritte Abtheilung. Zur Philosophie. Sechster Band*, III.6, *Psychologie*, ed. L. George (Berlin: G. Reimer, 1862), 27–28.

41. Friedrich Schleiermacher, *Dialektik* (1822), Band 2, ed. Manfred Frank (Berlin: Suhrkamp Verlag, 2001), 260.

42. Schleiermacher does not seem to have anywhere presented a comprehensive description of his views about finite causality. His views about causality continue to elicit robust disagreements between scholars. See, for example, the

differences between the interpretations in Dole, *Schleiermacher on Religion*, chap. 1, and Jacqueline Mariña, *Transformation of the Self in the Thought of Friedrich Schleiermacher* (Oxford: Oxford University Press, 2008). My view that Schleiermacher describes a form of causal determinism in *Christian Faith* (1830–31) may differ from the view of my colleague Anette Hagan, who provides a longer treatment of the topic in her chapter in this volume. However, I heartily agree with Hagan on what for our larger conversation in this volume seems the more important point— namely, that Schleiermacher's view supports strong activism.

43. *CF* §49.1, pp. 274–75.

44. For more about Schleiermacher's natural nexus and its import for his doctrine of providence, see chap. 4 from Anette Hagan in this volume.

45. *CF* §164.1, p. 999; §164.2, pp. 1000–1001.

46. *CF* §54.4, p. 310. "For everything that happens temporally and spatially also has its conditions in the totality of what is outside it and before it, however much these factors might be hidden from us thus far." See also §46.2, p. 253: "natural causation, viewed as the complete conditionality of all that happens through the general interconnected process of nature."

47. *CF* §54.1, p. 306. "Every single thing that is caused within the interconnected process of nature is also the unalloyed result of every entity that is causative within the interconnected process of nature, this in proportion to how it stands in relation to each one." See also §46.2, p. 253: "Within the totality of finite being only a particular and partial causality befits each individual item, in that each is dependent not on *one* other item but on *all other* items; general causality exists only in that source whereupon the totality of this divided causality is itself dependent." See also §47.2, p. 262: "all effectual causes working in accord to bring about this effect."

48. Immanuel Kant, *Critique of the Power of Judgment*, ed. Paul Guyer, trans. Paul Guyer and Eric Matthews (Cambridge: Cambridge University Press, 2000), 233–34, 250–51, 322. For Kant's description of what he calls "organized beings"— viz., organisms—see esp. 242–49. For a brief and accessible account of how several thinkers in Schleiermacher's generation criticized Kant's view and argued that the world *is* an organism, see Frederick C. Beiser, *The Romantic Imperative: The Concept of Early German Romanticism* (Cambridge, MA: Harvard University Press, 2003), esp. chap. 9, "Kant and the *Naturphilosophen*," 153–70.

49. Schleiermacher, *Dialectic*, 5.

50. Friedrich Schleiermacher, *Lectures on Philosophical Ethics*, ed. Robert B. Louden, trans. Louise Adey Huish (Cambridge: Cambridge University Press, 2002), 148–49.

51. Ibid., 149.

52. Friedrich Schleiermacher, "Über den Unterschied zwischen Naturgesetz und Sittengesetz," *KGA* I.11, ed. Martin Rößler (Berlin: de Gruyter, 2002), 447; for another place in Schleiermacher's oeuvre where he comments briefly on the major classes of existents, see Sämmtliche Werke III.6, 27–28, and *Schleiermachers Vorlesungen über die Aesthetik vorgetragen Ao. 1832–1833* (Nachlass Alexander Schweizer), available on the Schleiermacher in Berlin 1808–1834 project website: http:// schleiermacher-in-berlin.bbaw.de/vorlesungen/detail.xql?id=prov_shf_hbq_2r.

53. Schleiermacher, "Über den Unterschied zwischen Naturgesetz und Sittengesetz," 448–50.

54. Ibid.

55. This is the description of human perfection that Schleiermacher ascribes to Christ. See *CF* §96.3, p. 590.

56. *CE* 139.

57. For Schleiermacher's introduction and initial explanation of this idea, see *CF* §89. He reaffirms it in several passages thereafter—e.g., §92.1, p. 562; §94.3, p. 579; §97.4, p. 605. The majority view in Christian theology has been that God became incarnate as a response to sin. There is a minority view—most strongly associated with John Duns Scotus—according to which God would have become incarnate even if our ancestors had not sinned. But Scotus believed that human being was already *actually* (and completely) created. I know of no other major Christian theologian besides Schleiermacher who claims that the creation of human being was not completed until Jesus appeared in history. In their chapters in this volume, Shelli M. Poe and Anette Hagan also note that Schleiermacher took Christ to be the completion of the creation of human nature.

58. *CF* §164.1, p. 999.

59. Friedrich Schleiermacher, *Pädagogik: Die Theorie der Erziehung von 1820/21 in einer Nachschrift*, ed. Christiane Ehrhardt and Wolfgang Virmond (Berlin: de Gruyter, 2008), 253. Translation mine.

60. Schleiermacher, *On Religion*, 44.

61. Schleiermacher, *Lectures on Philosophical Ethics*, 17.

62. Ibid., 25; Friedrich Schleiermacher, "Über den Begriff des höchsten Gutes. Zweite Abhandlung," *KGA* I.11, ed. Martin Rößler (Berlin: de Gruyter, 2002), 672; Schleiermacher, *On Religion*, 92.

63. Friedrich Schleiermacher, "Über die Begriffe der verschiedenen Staatsformen," in *KGA* I.11, ed. Martin Rößler (Berlin: de Gruyter, 2002), 110, 113, 111, 118–19.

64. Schleiermacher, *On Religion*, 76–77. The impulse of religious communication is self-organizing, and the multiplicity of specific fellowships forms an indivisible, living whole.

65. Ibid., 40, 43, 44.

66. For more about Schleiermacher's conception of the church, see James M. Brandt's chap. 1 in this volume.

67. Friedrich Schleiermacher, *Christian Caring: Selections from* Practical Theology, ed. James O. Duke and Howard Stone, trans. James O. Duke (Philadelphia: Fortress Press, 1988), 103. Here it is important to note how Schleiermacher integrated his views about causality and his claim that individuals and groups are organisms within the larger world-organism. On Schleiermacher's view, social organisms are real causal agents, rather than merely figurative personifications or aggregated individual agents. A striking example of how this affects his causal narratives in *Christian Faith* is his claim that there is "a prototype within an individual psyche," which "even if it is not to be comprehended based on the previous states of that very psyche, would still have to be capable of being comprehended based on the force of the society [Volkskraft] to which that individual belongs" (translation revised slightly). *CF* postscript to §10, p. 78; CG postscript to §10, p. 92.

68. *CF* §96.3, p. 69. CG 69: "Nämlich das Sein Gottes in dem Erlöser ist als seine innerste Grundkraft gesezt von welcher alle Thätigkeit ausgeht, und welche all Momente zusammenhält; alles menschliche aber bildet nur den Organismus für diese Grundkraft, und verhält sich zu derselben beides als ihr aufnehmendes

und als ihr darstellendes System, so wie in uns alle andere Kräfte sich zur Intelligenz verhalten sollen."

69. *CF* §96.3, p. 590 (translation revised slightly).

70. On the relation of Christ to the church and to individual believers, *CF* §100.2, p. 625; to the rest of humanity, *CF* §97.4, pp. 605–6; §106.1, p. 684; to Scriptures, *CF* §130.2, p. 844.

71. *CF* §13.1, p. 95. "Only *Christ* is in a position gradually to enliven the entire human race to its higher state."

72. *CF* §92.1, p. 562.

73. *CF* §100.2, p. 624.

74. *CF* §94.3, p. 580.

75. H. Paul Santmire, an early and important voice in Christian ecotheological thinking, defines ecotheology in terms of this emphasis on conceiving the world as an "interrelated system." See "Ecotheology," in *Encyclopedia of Science and Religion*, vol. 1, *A–I*, ed. J. Wentzel Vrede van Huyssteen (New York: Macmillan Reference USA, 2003), 247–51.

76. See, for example: Rosemary Radford Ruether, *Gaia and God: An Ecofeminist Theology of Earth Healing* (New York: HarperCollins, 1992); Eileen Crist and H. Bruce Rinker, "One Grand Organic Whole," in *Gaia in Turmoil: Climate Change, Biodepletion, and Earth Ethics in a Time of Crisis*, ed. Eileen Crist and H. Bruce Rinker (Cambridge, MA: MIT Press, 2009), 1–5.

77. Jane Bennett, *Vibrant Matter: A Political Ecology of Things* (Durham, NC: Duke University Press, 2010), 1–38. For excellent introductions to forms of new materialism, see Diana Coole and Samantha Frost, eds., *New Materialisms: Ontology, Agency, and Politics* (Durham, NC: Duke University Press, 2010), 1–43; and Rick Dolphijn and Iris van der Tuin, eds., *New Materialism: Interviews and Cartographies* (Ann Arbor, MI: Open Humanities Press, 2012).

4. DIVINE PROVIDENCE AND HUMAN FREEDOM IN THE QUEST FOR ECOLOGICAL LIVING

1. David Fergusson, "Predestination: A Scottish Perspective," *Scottish Journal of Theology* 46, no. 4 (1993): 476.

2. See Christoph Schwöbel, "Divine Agency and Providence," *Modern Theology* 3, no. 3 (1987): 225.

3. *CF* §119.1, p. 780.

4. Colin E. Gunton, "The Doctrine of Creation," in *Cambridge Companion to Christian Doctrine*, ed. Colin E. Gunton (Cambridge: Cambridge University Press, 1997), 153.

5. In §58.3 in the context of the perfection of the world, and in §164.3 in relation to the Christian church as the object of divine government.

6. This term does not mean mere foreknowledge. Its meaning is much closer to foreordination. *Etwas versehen* means to make sure that something happens.

7. *CF* §164.3, p. 1002.

8. See *CF* §§46–49.

9. See Van A. Harvey, "A Word in Defense of Schleiermacher's Theological Method," *Journal of Religion* 42, no. 3 (1962): 164.

10. See Andrew Dole, *Schleiermacher on Religion and the Natural Order* (New York: Oxford University Press, 2010), 155.

11. Cf. *CF* postscript to §53, p. 304.

12. *CF* §54.4, p. 310.

13. The doctrine of God is therefore only completed by the end of the work. Cf. *CF* §31.2, p. 186.

14. Cf. *CF* §51.1, p. 290.

15. See Schwöbel, "Divine Agency and Providence," 232.

16. Michael Root, "Schleiermacher as Innovator and Inheritor: God, Dependence and Election," *Scottish Journal of Theology* 43, no. 1 (1990): 97.

17. See Edwin van Driel, "Schleiermacher's Supralapsarian Christology," *Scottish Journal of Theology* 60, no. 3 (2007): 254.

18. *CF* §46.2, p. 253.

19. *CF* §54.1, pp. 306–7.

20. Colin Gunton, "Election and Ecclesiology in the Post-Constantinian Church," *Scottish Journal of Theology* 53, no. 2 (2000): 214.

21. B. L. Hebblethwaite, "Some Reflections on Predestination, Providence and Divine Foreknowledge," *Religious Studies* 15, no. 4 (1979): 436.

22. See Schwöbel, "Divine Agency and Providence," 228.

23. Richard R. Niebuhr, *Schleiermacher on Christ and Religion* (New York: Charles Scribner's Sons, 1964), 257.

24. Ibid.

25. J. R. Lucas, "Foreknowledge," in *Philosophy in Christianity*, ed. G. Vesey (Cambridge: Cambridge University Press, 1989), 122.

26. *CF* §164.1, pp. 999–1000.

27. *CF* §32.1, p. 188.

28. *CF* §32.1, p. 187.

29. Robert Sherman, *The Shift to Modernity: Christ and the Doctrine of Creation in the Theologies of Schleiermacher and Barth* (New York: T&T Clark, 2005), 17.

30. See *CF* §4.4, p. 24.

31. *CF* §4.4, p. 26.

32. Matthias Gockel, *Barth and Schleiermacher on the Doctrine of Election* (New York: Oxford University Press, 2006), 43.

33. Bruce L. Boyer, "Schleiermacher on the Divine Causality," *Religious Studies* 22, no. 1 (1986): 117.

34. See *CF* §34, p. 198.

35. See Schwöbel, "Divine Agency and Providence," 239.

36. Eilert Herms, "Schleiermachers Eschatologie nach der zweiten Auflage der Glaubenslehre," in *Menschsein im Werden: Studien zu Schleiermacher* (Tübingen: Mohr Siebeck, 2003), 127.

37. See *CF* §36, p. 205.

38. See Anette I. Hagan, *Eternal Blessedness for All? A Historical-Systematic Examination of Friedrich Schleiermacher's Reinterpretation of Predestination* (Eugene, OR: Pickwick Publications, 2013), 179–80.

39. Sherman, *Shift to Modernity*, 118.

40. Ibid., 2.

41. *CF* §40.3, p. 220.

42. Martin Redeker, introduction to *Der christliche Glaube nach den Grundsätzen der evangelischen Kirche im Zusammenhange dargestellt*, ed. Martin Redeker, 2 vols., 7th ed., based on 2nd ed. of 1830–31 (Berlin: Walter de Gruyter, 1960), xxiv.

43. *CF* §46, pp. 247–48.

44. See*CF* §46.2, p. 253.

45. See Boyer, "Schleiermacher on the Divine Causality," 116. Boyer takes "system" from the 1928 translation of *Christian Faith*. The original German version has *Zusammenhang*.

46. Dole, *Schleiermacher on Religion*, 151.

47. *CF* postscript to §46, p. 256.

48. *CF* §46.2, p. 253.

49. Boyer, "Schleiermacher on the Divine Causality," 121.

50. See Root, "Schleiermacher as Innovator and Inheritor," 92.

51. See John P. Crossley Jr., "The Ethical Impulse in Schleiermacher's Early Ethics," *Journal of Religious Ethics* 34, no. 4 (2006): 601.

52. Schleiermacher makes only the general distinction between natural evils and human evils. The latter kind he terms "social," whether jointly or individually exercised. See *CF* §48.1, p. 266.

53. Dawn DeVries and Brian Gerrish, "Providence and Grace: Schleiermacher on Justification and Election," in *Cambridge Companion to Friedrich Schleiermacher*, ed. Jacqueline Mariña (Cambridge: Cambridge University Press, 2005), 195.

54. See *CF* §49.1, p. 272.

55. Sherman, *Shift to Modernity*, 162.

56. Karl Barth, *Protestant Theology in the Nineteenth Century: Its Background and History* (London: SCM Press, 2001), 421. Schleiermacher's own outlook on history and development entailed a possible consummate *telos* only between Christianized communities of faith and a theology that could affirm harmony with philosophical and scientific wisdom concerning human beings and the natural world as a whole. Reaching this goal would be a far cry from the secular progress and accomplishment of "civilization" that Barth applied to him. Schleiermacher's claim was only on behalf of God's activity among those growing in sanctification, which could eventually occur among all human beings in Christ. In between now and then, he prophetically foresaw a process of advancement in God-consciousness, sometimes infinitesimally small, sometimes wavering, but also declaring that in God's own way God would continue to provide impetus for a process of growth encapsulating all humanity. To be fulfilled, on Schleiermacher's account, this process may have to continue beyond death.

57. See Sherman, *Shift to Modernity*, 174.

58. *CF* §58.2, p. 343.

59. *CF* §59.1, p. 348.

60. *CF* §59.1, p. 348.

61. Dawn DeVries, "Schleiermacher," in *Blackwell Companion to Modern Theology*, ed. Gareth Jones (Oxford: Blackwell, 2007), 320.

62. Cf. *CF* §108.6, p. 709.

63. *CF* postscript to §59, p. 355.

64. See Hagan, *Eternal Blessedness for All*, 203.

65. *CF* §47.1, p. 260.

66. *CF* §109.3, p. 718.

67. *CF* §94.2, p. 578.

68. *CF* §93.3, p. 569.

69. *CF* §89.3, p. 556.

70. Chap. 3 offers a discussion of this possibility.

71. Sherman, *Shift to Modernity*, 151.

72. *CF* §100.2, p. 624.
73. *CF* §164.2, p. 1000.

5. SOCIAL SIN AND THE CULTIVATION OF NATURE

1. Friedrich Schleiermacher, "Christ the Liberator," in *Servant of the Word: Selected Sermons of Friedrich Schleiermacher*, trans. Dawn DeVries (Philadelphia: Fortress Press, 1987), 55. See also "Witnesses to the Resurrection," ibid., 73–84.
2. Schleiermacher, "Christ the Liberator," 55.
3. On Schleiermacher's innovative treatment of eschatology and the after-life, see chaps. 1 and 2.
4. Thus Schleiermacher speaks in his touching sermon at the graveside of his nine-year-old son Nathanael, "Sermon at Nathanael's Grave," in *Servant of the Word*, 211. Here, too, he affirms, redemption in Christ culminates not in an indi-vidual's escape from the ills of this world to heaven but in the reign of God over this created world.
5. Schleiermacher, "Christ the Liberator," 44.
6. See, for example, the critiques of Schleiermacher's doctrine of sin in Karl Barth, *Church Dogmatics*, III/3, *The Doctrine of Creation*, ed. G. W. Bromiley and T. F. Torrance (London: T&T Clark International, 2004), 319–34; and in Reinhold Niebuhr, *The Nature and Destiny of Man*, vol. 1 (Louisville, KY: Westminster John Knox Press, 1996), 245–48.
7. *CF* §68, p. 684; *CG* 412.
8. *CF* §98.1, p. 609.
9. *CF* §63, p. 385. Thus, sin is not known in and of itself; its character is dis-tinguished in the light of divine grace.
10. *CF* §71.2, p. 428.
11. *CF* §78.3, p. 488.
12. On this point, see Ernst M. Conradie, "Towards an Ecological Reformu-lation of the Christian Doctrine of Sin," *Journal of Theology for Southern Africa* 122 (2005): 4–5.
13. This dualism between humanity and nature is underscored in the influ-ential essay by Lynn White Jr., "The Historical Roots of Our Ecological Crisis," *Science* 155, no. 3767 (March 1967): 1203–7.
14. See Matthew Fox, *Original Blessing* (New York: Tarcher Perigee, 2000), 3.
15. For a more detailed analysis of Schleiermacher's social conception of sin, see Kevin M. Vander Schel, "Friedrich Schleiermacher," in *T&T Clark Companion to the Doctrine of Sin*, ed. Keith L. Johnson and David Lauber (New York: Bloomsbury T&T Clark, 2016), 251–66.
16. On this point, see *CF* §§11.2 and 14.2.
17. *CF* §63, p. 385; *CG* 394–95.
18. See *CF* §§79–82 and 59–61. In this respect, both sin and evil remain depen-dent upon the eternal divine causality. As Schleiermacher affirms, all that hap-pens and "all that is real" without exception is wholly dependent upon God (§48.3). While neither sin in itself nor evil as such is directly willed by God, then, still Schleiermacher maintains that sin must in some way subsist through the divine causality (§79.1). Thus, in contrast with traditional creedal formulations,

Schleiermacher argues that to recognize God as the author of redemption also entails, in this limited and specific sense, acknowledging God as the "author" of sin (§79). On the theme of God as "author" of sin, see also Schleiermacher, *On the Doctrine of Election, with Special Reference to the Aphorisms of Dr. Bretschneider*, trans. Iain G. Nicol and Allen G. Jorgenson, Columbia Series in Reformed Theology (Louisville, KY: Westminster John Knox Press, 2006), 67–73; and Matthias Gockel, *Barth and Schleiermacher on the Doctrine of Election* (New York: Oxford University Press, 2006), 63–67.

19. *CF* §72.4, p. 445; *CG* 449. See also §72.5.

20. *CF* §66.1, p. 403.

21. *CF* §71.4, p. 432; §72.5, p. 449.

22. *CF* §69.1, p. 413.

23. *CF* §71.2, p. 428.

24. *CF* §71, pp. 424–25; *CG* 427.

25. *CF* postscript to §69, p. 416.

26. *CF* §71.1, p. 427; *CG* 428. As Schleiermacher makes clear, it belongs to the nature of this diseased condition that it is constantly issuing forth in action: "In all human beings actual sin is continually issuing from original sin" (§73, p. 454).

27. See Friedrich Schleiermacher, "Christ Is Like Us in All Things but Sin," in *Schleiermacher: Christmas Dialogue, The Second Speech, and Other Selections*, ed. and trans. Julia A. Lamm (New York: Paulist Press, 2014), 244; and *CF* §71.1.

28. *CF* §73.1, p. 455.

29. *CF* §71.2, p. 430.

30. It is in this sense that Christ, who suffered great misfortune at the hands of others, is yet without sin. See Schleiermacher, "Christ Is Like Us," 241–49.

31. See *CF* §75, p. 473.

32. *CF* §76.1, p. 479.

33. *CF* §75.1, p. 475.

34. *CF* §75.1, p. 475.

35. *CF* §75.2, p. 476; *CG* 473–74.

36. *CF* §76, p. 478; *CG* 475.

37. *CF* §76.3, p. 482; *CG* 479.

38. *CF* §77.1, p. 483.

39. *CF* §84.2, p. 527; *CG* 521.

40. See *CF* §77.1.

41. On the revisionist character of Schleiermacher's treatment of sin, see Walter E. Wyman Jr., "Rethinking the Christian Doctrine of Sin: Friedrich Schleiermacher and Hick's 'Irenaean Type,'" *Journal of Religion* 74, no. 2 (1994): 119–217. However, the differences between Schleiermacher's analysis and more traditional Augustinian conceptions of sin should not be overstated. As Brian Gerrish notes: "There is a good deal of Augustine and Calvin in Schleiermacher." See Brian A. Gerrish, *Christian Faith: Dogmatics in Outline* (Louisville, KY: Westminster John Knox Press, 2015), 102.

42. On the themes of structural sin and structural violence, see esp. Gustavo Gutiérrez, *A Theology of Liberation: History, Politics, and Salvation*, trans. and ed. Sr. Caridad Inda and John Eagleson (Maryknoll, NY: Orbis Books, 1986), 145–88; Rosemary Radford Ruether, *Sexism and God-Talk: Toward a Feminist Theology* (Boston: Beacon Press, 1983), 159–92; and Elisabeth Schüssler Fiorenza, *Wisdom Ways: Introducing Feminist Biblical Interpretation* (Maryknoll, NY: Orbis Books, 2001), 102–34.

For discussion of Schleiermacher's understanding of social sin as anticipating these recent trends of social criticism within theology, see Rick Elgendy, "Reconsidering Resurrection, Incarnation, and Nature in Schleiermacher's *Glaubenslehre*," *International Journal of Systematic Theology* 15, no. 3 (2013): 302, 311–13; and cf. Joerg Rieger, *Christ and Empire* (Minneapolis: Fortress Press, 2007), 197–236; and Derek R. Nelson, *What's Wrong with Sin? Sin in Individual and Social Perspective from Schleiermacher to Theologies of Liberation* (Edinburgh: T&T Clark, 2009), 15–48. Schleiermacher's analysis of sin also proved influential for Kierkegaard's discussion of repentance and for Walter Rauschenbusch's later development of the social gospel. See Walter Rauschenbusch, *Theology for the Social Gospel* (Louisville, KY: Westminster John Knox Press, 1997), 27, 92–93; and Richard E. Crouter, "Schleiermacher: Revisiting Kierkegaard's Relationship to Him," in *Kierkegaard and His German Contemporaries*, vol. 2, ed. Jon Stewart (London: Ashgate Publishing, 2007), 197–232, esp. 215–18.

43. The topic of ecological sin has been a growing point of focus in recent theological discussion. See, for example, William H. Becker, "Ecological Sin," *Theology Today* 49, no. 2 (July 1992): 152–64; Conradie, "Towards an Ecological Reformulation"; and Peter Heinegg, "The Ecological Curse: A Reading of Genesis 3," *CrossCurrents* 65, no. 4 (December 2015): 441–47.

44. Perhaps the best known of these garbage patches is the Great Pacific Garbage Patch, which stretches across the North Pacific Subtropical Gyre. Charles Moore discovered this widespread collection of marine debris in 1997 and subsequently began the Algalita Marine Research Foundation to study its growth and effects. His account is detailed in Charles Moore and Cassandra Phillips, *Plastic Oceans: How a Sea Captain's Chance Discovery Launched a Determined Quest to Save the Oceans* (New York: Penguin Press, 2011). In a subsequent 2014 expedition, which utilized aerial drones to more accurately measure the scale of the waste, Moore found concentrations of plastic debris significantly larger than previous estimates, as well as semipermanent plastic "islands." See Charles J. Moore, "Choking the Oceans with Plastic," *New York Times*, August 25, 2014, http://www.nytimes.com /2014/08/26/opinion/choking-the-oceans-with-plastic.html?ref=opinion&_r=3. For discussion of the distribution, composition, and long-term effects of marine debris, see the essays of Melanie Bergmann, Lars Gutow, and Michael Klages, eds., *Marine Anthropogenic Litter* (New York: Springer International Publishing, 2015). For estimates of the size and range of this marine debris, see Peter G. Ryan et al., "Monitoring the Abundance of Plastic Debris in the Marine Environment," *Philosophical Transactions of the Royal Society B: Biological Sciences* 364, no. 1526 (2009): 1999–2012.

45. See François Galgani, Georg Hanke, and Thomas Maes, "Global Distribution, Composition and Abundance of Marine Litter," in Bergmann, Gutow, and Klages, *Marine Anthropogenic Litter*, 30. The presence of floating plastic litter has been recorded even in remote oceans, such as the Arctic and Antarctic (40).

46. For the widespread impact of marine litter upon marine life, see Susanne Kühn, Elisa L. Bravo Rebolledo, and Jan A. van Graneker, "Deleterious Effects of Litter on Marine Life," in Bergmann, Gutow, and Klages, *Marine Anthropogenic Litter*, 75–116, esp. 85–96. For a discussion of the impact of marine plastics on human health, see Tamara S. Galloway, "Micro- and Nano-plastics and Human Health," in *Marine Anthropogenic Litter*, 343–66, esp. 351–58.

47. See US Government Accountability Office's 2008 report "Electronic Waste: EPA Needs to Better Control Harmful U.S. Exports through Stronger Enforcement

and More Comprehensive Regulation," https://www.gao.gov/products/GAO-08-1044; and "The E-Waste Problem," Greenpeace, http://www.greenpeace.org/international/en/campaigns/detox/electronics/the-e-waste-problem/.

48. John Steinbeck's chronicle of the Joad family in *The Grapes of Wrath* (New York: Viking Press, 1939) offers a vivid portrayal of the hardships caused by these dust storms. For an overview of the causes of these storms in the region, as well as personal accounts of the worst storms of the 1930s, see R. Douglas Hurt, *The Dust Bowl: An Agricultural and Social History* (Chicago: Nelson Hall, 1981). For further analysis of the connections between the Dust Bowl and the Great Depression, see Brad D. Lookingbill, *Dust Bowl, USA: Depression America and the Ecological Imagination, 1929–1941* (Athens: Ohio University Press, 2001).

49. See Hurt, *Dust Bowl*, 50–51; and Lookingbill, *Dust Bowl, USA*, 14–15.

50. See Hurt, *Dust Bowl*, 2; and Lookingbill, *Dust Bowl, USA*, 25–26. Hurt's volume begins with an account of a local church holding a special rain service to plead for divine aid in ending the drought.

51. On the rapid settlement of this region and the enticing descriptions of this new and promising "frontier," see Lookingbill, *Dust Bowl, USA*, 7–23, esp. 17–20. The phrase "rain follows the plow," popularized by Charles Dana Wilber in his 1881 book *The Great Valleys and Prairies of Nebraska and the Northwest*, became a slogan for the climatological belief that agricultural cultivation would gradually yield a fundamental change in weather patterns. See Gary D. Libecap and Zeynep Kocabiyik Hansen, "'Rain Follows the Plow' and Dryfarming Doctrine: The Climate Information Problem and Homestead Failure in the Upper Great Plains, 1890–1925," *Journal of Economic History* 62, no. 1 (2002): 86–120.

52. See Hurt, *Dust Bowl*, 6–10.

53. David Bentley Hart's *The Doors of the Sea* (Grand Rapids: Wm. B. Eerdmans Publishing Co., 2005) provides a poignant reflection on the theological ramifications of this tsunami and its aftermath. The earthquake itself, with an estimated magnitude of 9.1–9.3, was the third largest ever recorded by seismograph, and the duration of the fault rupture was the longest ever recorded. See Thorne Lay et al., "The Great Sumatra-Andaman Earthquake of 26 December 2004," and Charles J. Ammon et al., "Rupture Process of the 2004 Sumatra-Andaman Earthquake," in *Science* 308, no. 5725 (May 20, 2005): 1127–33 and 1133–39.

54. The 2012 film *The Impossible* was based on the experience of Spanish physician María Belón and her family while on vacation in Thailand. Leading actress Naomi Watts was nominated for Golden Globe and Academy Awards for her performance.

55. At the time the tsunami struck, for example, both Indonesia and Sri Lanka had been long affected by protracted and bloody civil conflicts. See Elizabeth Ferris, "Natural Disaster and Conflict-Induced Displacement: Similarities, Differences, and Inter-Connections," in *Environmental Protection and Human Rights*, ed. Donald K. Anton and Dinah L. Shelton (New York: Cambridge University Press, 2011), 666–70.

56. See Rhona MacDonald, "How Women Were Affected by the Tsunami: A Perspective from Oxfam," *PLoS Medicine* 2, no. 6 (June 28, 2005), doi:10.1371/journal.pmed.0020178.

57. Accordingly, apart from sin, social evils would only provide incentives or occasions toward further spiritual action. See *CF* §77.2–3.

58. See *CF* §77.2.

59. On this correspondence between the "collective life of sin" and the "collective life of grace," see *CF* §88.4, p. 552–53.

60. *CF* §87, p. 544.

61. *CF* §§89.1–2 and 106.2.

62. *CF* §106.1, p. 683.

63. *CF* §110.1, p. 722.

64. See *CF* §112.1–2 and §110.1–2.

65. On the relation of Schleiermacher's *Christian Faith* and *Christian Ethics*, see *CF* §§78.1, 112.5, and 126.2. On the organization and structure of Schleiermacher's *Christian Ethics*, see chap. 2, above, 44–55.

66. Peiter, 96. All translations from this text are by the author.

67. For a more detailed discussion of these three forms of distinctively Christian action, see James Brandt's chapter in the present volume, as well as Brandt, *All Things New: Reform of Church and Society in Schleiermacher's* Christian Ethics (Louisville, KY: Westminster John Knox Press, 2001), 109–34; and Kevin M. Vander Schel, *Embedded Grace: Christ, History, and the Reign of God in Schleiermacher's Dogmatics* (Minneapolis: Fortress Press, 2013), 168–79, 190–219.

68. Peiter, 97.

69. See Peiter, 94–98, 109. On the prophetic character of purifying action, see also Brandt, *All Things New*, 119–24.

70. In this respect, broadening action also displays both inner and outer aspects. On the inner/outer distinction in Schleiermacher's *Christian Ethics*, see chap. 2 above.

71. Peiter, 269.

72. On the correspondence of talent and virtue in Schleiermacher's Christian ethics, see Peiter, 265.

73. This immanent and subtle transformation of the created and natural world corresponds to the larger theme of the "supernatural-becoming-natural" (*Naturwerden des Übernatürlichen*) in Schleiermacher's mature theology. On the centrality of this motif within Schleiermacher's *Christian Faith* and lectures on Christian ethics, see Vander Schel, *Embedded Grace*, 8–11, 39–43, 83–86.

74. Peiter, 444.

75. Ibid.

76. Schleiermacher does not regard civil society, for instance, as a necessary political compromise for the sake of justice or protection but presents the civil condition as "precisely the consolidation [*Vereinigung*] of powers for the dominion over nature [*zur Beherrschung der Natur*]." See Peiter, 444.

77. See Gerrish, *Christian Faith: Dogmatics in Outline*, 94–95. For a discussion of the antithesis of nature and spirit in Ritschl's thought, and the curiously central role it has played in the Anglophone reception of Schleiermacher's theology, see Christine Helmer, *Theology and the End of Doctrine* (Louisville, KY: Westminster John Knox Press, 2014), 23–57.

78. Peiter, 446 n. 2. This same note continues: "The cultivation of nature is cultivation for the Spirit [*Die Bildung der Natur ist Bildung für den Geist*]."

79. On the theme of ecological living as "being at home on earth," see Ernst Conradie, *An Ecological Christian Anthropology: At Home on Earth?* (New York: Ashgate Publishing, 2005), 1–22.

80. See, for instance, John Calvin's rich commentary on Gen. 2:15: "The earth was given to man [*sic*], with this condition, that he should occupy himself in its

cultivation. Whence it follows that men were created to employ themselves in some work, and not to lie down in inactivity and idleness . . . The custody of the garden was given in charge to Adam, to show that we possess the things which God has committed to our hands, on the condition, that being content with a frugal and moderate use of them, we should take care of what shall remain. Let him who possesses a field, so partake of its yearly fruits, that he may not suffer the ground to be injured by his negligence; but let him endeavor to hand it down to posterity as he received it, or even better cultivated. . . . Let every one regard himself as the steward of God in all things which he possesses. Then he will neither conduct himself dissolutely, nor corrupt by abuse those things which God requires to be preserved." See Calvin, *Commentaries on the Book of Genesis*, vol. 1, trans. John King (Grand Rapids: Baker Book House, 1981), 125.

81. Peiter, 475, 481. Schleiermacher's lectures on Christian ethics thus present no attempt to accommodate the redemptive work of Christ to cultural and social progress but point to the permeation and elevation of human action in the natural world through the Spirit. In the words of the lectures: "In a civil society which consists of Christians, the primary communal purpose of all should be communal movement toward perfection in the reign of God" (444).

82. See Conradie, *Ecological Christian Anthropology*, 2, 10.

83. See, for example, the essays in John Chryssavgis and Bruce V. Foltz, eds., *Toward an Ecology of Transfiguration: Orthodox Christian Perspectives on Environment, Nature, and Creation* (New York: Fordham University Press, 2013); Elizabeth Theokritoff, *Living in God's Creation: Orthodox Perspectives on Ecology* (Crestwood, NY: St. Vladimir's Seminary Press, 2009); and Ecumenical Patriarch Bartholomew, *On Earth as in Heaven: Ecological Vision and Initiatives of Ecumenical Patriarch Bartholomew* (New York: Fordham University Press, 2011).

84. See Ilia Delio's innovative recovery of the theme of "catholicity" in *Making All Things New: Catholicity, Cosmology, Consciousness* (Maryknoll, NY: Orbis Books, 2015); see also Pope Francis, *Laudato Si': On Care for Our Common Home* (Huntington, IN: Our Sunday Visitor, 2015).

85. See, for example, Conradie, *Ecological Christian Anthropology*, esp. 79–182. See also Jürgen Moltmann, *God in Creation: A New Theology of Creation and the Spirit of God*, trans. Margaret Kohl (San Francisco: Harper & Row, 1985); Colin E. Gunton, *Christ and Creation* (Carlisle, UK: Paternoster Press, 1992); and Colin E. Gunton, *The One, the Three, and the Many: God, Creation, and the Culture of Modernity* (New York: Cambridge University Press, 1993).

CONCLUSION

1. For a brief account of how Schleiermacher progressed toward being a theologian, a summary of his major doctrines, and exact definitions of terms, see Terrence Tice, *Schleiermacher* (Nashville: Abingdon Press, 2006). For Schleiermacher's overview of the nature and task of theology, see his *Brief Outline of Theology as a Field of Study*, 3rd ed. (Louisville, KY: Westminster John Knox Press, 2011). For an intellectual history of his background for becoming a "political activist," see Theodore Vial, *Schleiermacher: A Guide for the Perplexed* (London: Bloomsbury T&T Clark, 2013). To explore his involvement with early German Romantics (1796–

1806) or to gain further insight into his philosophical work as a critical realist, see Hans Dierkes, Terrence N. Tice, and Wolfgang Virmond, eds., *Schleiermacher, Romanticism, and the Critical Arts: A Festschrift in Honor of Hermann Patsch* (Lewiston, NY: Edwin Mellen Press, 2008).

2. Over many decades, two poets have captured this reality and God's creative and redemptive presence within it, in a strongly contemplative spirit like Schleiermacher's. For fifty years Wendell Berry has farmed his land to provide food for his family by ecologically sensitive means. His poetry is often cited by others bearing like concerns for the environment. See his latest collection of poetry, offered year by year, 1979–2013: *This Day: Collected and New Sabbath Poems* (Berkeley, CA: Counterpoint, 2013), xxvii. In a different vein, Mary Oliver, using fewer words and not so much regarding environmental concerns as directly partaking of what nature gives us, day by day, has written during a similar period, also into old age, but also of a deeply attentive, contemplative spirit. See her latest volume, *Felicity* (New York: Penguin Press, 2016). See also any of her previous volumes of poetry, including her two volumes of *New and Selected Poems* (Boston: Beacon Press, 1992–2005). Both poets have drawn from Christian sources. In a Schleiermacher-type introduction to his 2013 work, Berry holds that what seems merely "natural" or especially "wild" to some has much to teach those who have despoiled or been complicit in degrading the land and its waters, activity that he takes to be truly, negatively "wild."

3. See esp. chaps. 1, 2, and 5, by James Brandt, Shelli Poe, and Kevin Vander Schel, which set up and flesh out parameters for traversing boundaries between doctrine and practices. See also Vander Schel, *Embedded Grace: Christ, History, and the Reign of God in Schleiermacher's Dogmatics* (Minneapolis: Fortress Press, 2013).

4. *CF* §12.2n8.

5. I know of no other work that has performed this service, though her recent research on his doctrine of "predestination" has surely paved the way. See Anette I. Hagan, *Eternal Blessedness for All? A Historical-Systematic Examination of Friedrich Schleiermacher's Reinterpretation of Predestination* (Eugene, OR: Pickwick Publications, 2013).

6. Naomi Klein is a keen-eyed reporter and gifted, communicative writer. Her book *This Changes Everything: Capitalism vs. the Climate* (New York: Simon & Schuster, 2014) is highly recommended later in this chapter. See her sequel, *No Is Not Enough: Resisting Trump's Shock Politics and Winning the World We Need* (Chicago: Haymarket Books, 2017).

7. I have critically presented this alternative approach in "The 'Schleiermacher Renaissance' Begins to Take Hold, Selectively, in American Thought and Life: Part 1: Prefatory Remarks on Secular, Apologetic, and Constructive Theology (Dewey, Knudson, and Brown)," chap. 18 of *Schleiermacher's Influences on American Thought and Religious Life, 1835–1920*, 3 vols., ed. Jeffrey Wilcox, Terrence Tice, and Catherine Kelsey (Eugene, OR: Wipf & Stock, 2013), 3:113–48, using the philosophical theology of Bordon Parker Bowne and Albert Knudson in Boston Personalism as prime examples. Elements of it are also to be found in the constructive theology of William Adams Brown. In contrast, John Dewey's "secular theology," drawn largely from Schleiermacher, builds his religious but purely secular accounts chiefly on empirical grounds.

8. See Leonardo Boff, *Ecology and Liberation: A New Paradigm*, trans. John Cumming (Maryknoll, NY: Orbis Books, 1993, in Portuguese; ET, 1995). See also

his closely associated, more noted work *Cry of the Earth, Cry of the Poor* (Maryknoll, NY: Orbis Books, 1995, in Portuguese, under the main title *Ecologia*; ET, using the original subtitle, 1997).

9. Cobb's book is very accessible. So is a fine book of ten essays edited by David Ray Griffin, *Spirituality and Society: Postmodern Visions* (Albany: State University of New York Press, 1988). Especially pertinent is an essay in that volume by economist Herman E. Daly, "The Steady-State Economy: Postmodern Alternative to Growthmania," 107–22. Further, a useful, more complex offering on this subject from Lutheran social ethicist Larry L. Rasmussen, then at Union Theological Seminary (New York), is his lengthy work *Earth Community, Earth Ethics* (Maryknoll, NY: Orbis Books, 1996). Dieter T. Hessel edited an indispensable volume of offerings from numerous, mostly theological disciplines in twenty chapters, plus an epilogue by Larry Rasmussen: *Theology for Earth Community: A Field Guide* (Maryknoll, NY: Orbis Books, 1996). The latter two books, and Cobb's *Sustainability*, are part of Orbis Books' Ecology and Justice series, which has contributed to the discussion since the 1990s. Among current work by meteorologists, climate scientists, and others, I have found Douglas Muschette's website to be highly informative: http://www.serioussustainability.org. He, too, was an early adopter of this concern.

10. On the high significance of love, see Ilia Delio, *Making All Things New: Catholicity, Cosmology, Consciousness* (Maryknoll, NY: Orbis Books, 2015), 162. Among recent studies on Schleiermacher, see also Steven R. Jungkeit, *Spaces of Modern Theology: Geography and Power in Schleiermacher's World* (New York: Palgrave Macmillan, 2012). In the concluding pages, he positively "finds" himself in the very "ruins" left by Schleiermacher.

11. It is available at Ann Arbor, MI: University Microfilms, 1970. The analysis still seems to hold up, especially in view of the continued highly entangled, differing usage of that term. Thus, I plan to reissue that study soon, with some alterations based on further extended inquiry.

12. For ways in which social contracts and tendencies have played distinct roles in much-studied denials of climate change and associated disasters and responsibilities for them, see Kari Marie Norgaard, *Living in Denial: Climate Change, Emotions, and Everyday Life* (Cambridge, MA: MIT Press, 2011).

13. I have not studied these various iterations.

14. Wilcox, Tice, and Kelsey, *Schleiermacher's Influences*, displays widespread evidence of Schleiermacher's influence on people across many ideological divides, including progressives such as John Dewey and the great African American Christian leaders Howard Thurman and Martin Luther King Jr. For several decades of his era and occasionally to this day, John Dewey, the great "pragmatist," was widely regarded as the quintessentially American philosopher.

15. For more than fifteen years up to 2016, *Christian Faith*, the greatest of Schleiermacher's masterpieces, was being prepared in a new translation and critical edition, which some of the present authors also examined in manuscript: Friedrich Schleiermacher, *Christian Faith*, trans. Terrence N. Tice, Catherine L. Kelsey, and Edwina Lawler, ed. Catherine L. Kelsey and Terrence N. Tice, 2 vols. (Louisville, KY: Westminster John Knox Press, 2016). See also Aaron J. Ghiloni, *John Dewey among the Theologians* (New York: Peter Lang, 2012).

16. See, for example, John Dewey, *Individualism Old and New* (1927; repr., New York: Capricorn Books, 1950). Howard Thurman and Martin Luther King Jr. would do so on like grounds and in similar fashion.

17. Robert Pollin, *Greening the Global Economy* (Cambridge, MA: MIT Press, 2015).

18. Alongside Naomi Klein's report, Jane Mayer's equally fine, thorough-going report on what she calls "the shadow economy," *Dark Money: The Hidden History of the Billionaires behind the Rise of the Radical Right* (New York: Doubleday, 2016), is to be highly recommended, for it puts together the forces of finance and politics in America, which have also had an enormous impact on climate change and the denial of it. Jane Mayer is still covering this beat. As a pictorial frontispiece, as it were, consult Barbara Kingsolver's foreword to and stories in *Thoreau's Legacy: American Stories about Global Warming*, ed. Richard Hayes (Cambridge, MA: Union of Concerned Scientists, 2009).

19. See *CF* §59.1 and §59 n. 9.

20. *CF* §78 n. 1, p. 486; §78.2, p. 487.

21. If anyone should be called an apostle of climate change, it could be Methodist layman Bill McKibben, when he first issued *The End of Nature* (New York: Random House, 1989; reissued, 2006). His title says what he means: Nature as we once knew it, an endless resource for energy and enjoyment, has long been slipping away. Even huge aquifers kept by the last glacier age are nearly depleted. Initially a writer on this subject for the *New Yorker*, he has continued to gather knowledge on it from hither and yon and now appears on behalf of nature on TV. For him, we humans are now irrefutably a part of nature. For the first time, the most prominent term for this fact, geographically speaking, is calling this period the Anthropocene Age. Jedediah Purdy uses this term in a work examining how we humans have been not only destroying the term "nature" but also constructing and destroying nature itself: *After Nature: A Politics for the Anthropocene* (Cambridge, MA: Harvard University Press, 2015).

22. It provides up-do-date information at www.ClimateRealityProject.org.

23. Get the revised edition of Rebecca J. Barnes, *50 Ways to Help Save the Earth: How You and Your Church Can Make a Difference* (Louisville, KY: Westminster John Knox Press, 2016), and don't forget to pick up Naomi Klein's exciting bestseller, *This Changes Everything*. Orbis Books has published a semipopular, more academic series since the early 1990s, Ecology and Justice, meant chiefly to stimulate thought but not yet containing an entire theological worldview as this volume does. Theological leader John Cobb started it off and continues to hold workshops annually. If you are interested in food and agriculture, contact the Land Institute (https://landinstitute.org/), headed by Wes Jackson, which has long been studying and experimenting with alternatives to current practices at its center in Salina, Kansas.

BIBLIOGRAPHY

Agyeman, Julian. "Sustainability." In *Keywords for Environmental Studies*, edited by Joni Adamson, William A. Gleason, and David N. Pellow, 186–89. New York: New York University Press, 2016.

Ammon, Charles J., Chen Ji, Hong-Kie Thio, David Robinson, Sidao Ni, Vala Hjorleifsdottir, Hiroo Kanamori, Thorne Lay, Shamita Das, Don Helmberger, Gene Ichinose, Jascha Polet, and David Wald. "Rupture Process of the 2004 Sumatra-Andaman Earthquake." *Science* 308, no. 5725 (May 20, 2005): 1133–39.

Barnes, Rebecca J. *50 Ways to Help Save the Earth: How You and Your Church Can Make a Difference*. Rev. ed. Louisville, KY: Westminster John Knox Press, 2016.

Barth, Karl. *Church Dogmatics*. Vol. III/1 and 3, *The Doctrine of Creation*. Translated by J. W. Edwards, O. Bussey, and H. Knight. Edited by G. W. Bromiley and T. F. Torrance. London: T&T Clark International, 2004.

———. *Protestant Theology in the Nineteenth Century: Its Background and History*. London: SCM Press, 2001.

———. *The Theology of Schleiermacher*. Edited by Dietrich Ritschl. Translated by Geoffrey W. Bromiley. Grand Rapids: Wm. B. Eerdmans Publishing Co., 1982.

Bartholomew, Ecumenical Patriarch. *On Earth as in Heaven: Ecological Vision and Initiatives of Ecumenical Patriarch Bartholomew*. New York: Fordham University Press, 2011.

Becker, William H. "Ecological Sin." *Theology Today* 49, no. 2 (July 1992): 152–64.

Beiser, Frederick C. *The Romantic Imperative: The Concept of Early German Romanticism*. Cambridge, MA: Harvard University Press, 2003.

Bennett, Jane. *Vibrant Matter: A Political Ecology of Things*. Durham, NC: Duke University Press, 2010.

Bergmann, Melanie, Lars Gutow, and Michael Klages, eds. *Marine Anthropogenic Litter*. New York: Springer International Publishing, 2015.

Berry, Wendell. *This Day: Collected and New Sabbath Poems*. Berkeley, CA: Counterpoint Press, 2013.

Bigler, Robert M. *The Politics of German Protestantism: The Rise of the Protestant Church Elite in Prussia, 1815–1848*. Berkeley: University of California Press, 1972.

Birkner, Hans-Joachim. *Schleiermachers christliche Sittenlehre im Zusammenhang seines philosophisch-theologischen Systems*. Theologische Bibliothek Töpelmann. Berlin: Alfred Töpelmann, 1964.

Boff, Leonardo. *Cry of the Earth, Cry of the Poor.* Maryknoll, NY: Orbis Books, 1997.

———. *Ecology and Liberation: A New Paradigm.* Translated by John Cumming. Maryknoll, NY: Orbis Books, 1995.

Boyd, George N. "Schleiermacher's 'Über den Unterschied zwischen Naturgesetz und Sittengesetz.'" *Journal of Religious Ethics* 17, no. 2 (Fall 1989): 41–49.

Boyer, Bruce L. "Schleiermacher on the Divine Causality." *Religious Studies* 22, no. 1 (1986): 113–23.

Brandt, James. *All Things New: Reform of Church and Society in Schleiermacher's Christian Ethics.* Louisville, KY: Westminster John Knox Press, 2001.

———. *Die Mystik und Das Wort: Der Gegensatz zwischen moderner Religionsauffassung und christlichen Glauben.* Tübingen: J. C. B. Mohr, 1924.

Brunner, Emil. *The Divine Imperative.* Translated by Olive Wyon. Philadelphia: Westminster Press, 1947.

Butler, Judith. *Undoing Gender.* New York: Routledge, 2004.

Calvin, John. *Commentaries on the Book of Genesis.* Vol. 1. Translated by John King. Grand Rapids: Baker Book House, 1981.

Chryssavgis, John, and Bruce V. Foltz, eds. *Toward an Ecology of Transfiguration: Orthodox Christian Perspectives on Environment, Nature, and Creation.* New York: Fordham University Press, 2013.

Coakley, Sarah. *Christ without Absolutes.* New York: Clarendon Press, 1995.

Cobb, John B., Jr. *Sustainability: Economics, Ecology, and Justice.* Maryknoll, NY: Orbis Books, 1992. Reissued, Eugene, OR: Wipf & Stock, 2007.

Coffey, David. *Deus Trinitatis: The Doctrine of the Triune God.* New York: Oxford University Press, 1999.

Conradie, Ernst M. *The Earth in God's Economy: Creation, Salvation and Consummation in Ecological Perspective.* Zurich: LIT Verlag, 2015.

———. *An Ecological Christian Anthropology: At Home on Earth?* New York: Ashgate Publishing, 2005.

———. "Towards an Ecological Reformulation of the Christian Doctrine of Sin." *Journal of Theology for Southern Africa* 122 (July 2005): 4–22.

Coole, Diana, and Samantha Frost, eds. *New Materialisms: Ontology, Agency, and Politics.* Durham, NC: Duke University Press, 2010.

Crist, Eileen, and H. Bruce Rinker. "One Grand Organic Whole." In *Gaia in Turmoil: Climate Change, Biodepletion, and Earth Ethics in a Time of Crisis,* edited by Eileen Crist and H. Bruce Rinker, 1–5. Cambridge, MA: MIT Press, 2009.

Crossley, John P., Jr. "The Ethical Impulse in Schleiermacher's Early Ethics." *Journal of Religious Ethics* 34, no. 4 (2006): 585–608.

Crouter, Richard E. "Schleiermacher: Revisiting Kierkegaard's Relationship to Him." In *Kierkegaard and His German Contemporaries* 2, edited by Jon Stewart. London: Ashgate Publishing, 2007.

Curran, Thomas H. *Doctrine and Speculation in Schleiermacher's Glaubenslehre.* New York: Walter de Gruyter, 1994.

Daly, Herman E. "The Steady-State Economy: Postmodern Alternative to Growthmania." In *Spirituality and Society: Postmodern Visions,* edited by

David Ray Griffin, 107–22. Albany: State University of New York Press, 1988.

Dauvergne, Peter. "The Problem of Consumption." *Global Environmental Politics* 10, no. 2 (2010): 1–10.

———. "Sustainability." In *Historical Dictionary of Environmentalism*, 195. 2nd ed. Lanham, MD: Rowman & Littlefield, 2016.

———. "The Sustainability Story: Exposing Truths, Half-Truths, and Illusions." In *New Earth Politics: Essays from the Anthropocene*, edited by Simon Nicholson and Sikina Jinnah, 387–404. Cambridge, MA: MIT Press, 2016.

Delio, Ilia. *Making All Things New: Catholicity, Cosmology, Consciousness.* Maryknoll, NY: Orbis Books, 2015.

DeVries, Dawn. *Jesus Christ in the Preaching of Calvin and Schleiermacher.* Louisville, KY: Westminster John Knox Press, 1996.

———. "Schleiermacher." In *Blackwell Companion to Modern Theology*, edited by Gareth Jones, 311–26. Oxford: Blackwell, 2007.

DeVries, Dawn, and Brian A. Gerrish. "Providence and Grace: Schleiermacher on Justification and Election." In *Cambridge Companion to Friedrich Schleiermacher*, edited by Jacqueline Mariña, 189–207. Cambridge: Cambridge University Press, 2005.

Dewey, John. *Individualism Old and New.* New York: Capricorn Books, 1950.

———. *Reconstruction in Philosophy.* New York: Mentor Books, 1950.

Dierkes, Hans, Terrence N. Tice, and Wolfgang Virmond, eds. *Schleiermacher, Romanticism, and the Critical Arts: A Festschrift in Honor of Hermann Patsch.* Lewiston, NY: Edwin Mellen Press, 2008.

Dilthey, Wilhelm. *Gesammelte Schriften.* V. 14, bd. 2. *Schleiermachers System als Philosophie und Theologie.* Leipzig: Teubner, 1985.

Dole, Andrew. *Schleiermacher on Religion and the Natural Order.* New York: Oxford University Press, 2010.

Dolphijn, Rick, and Iris van der Tuin, eds. *New Materialism: Interviews and Cartographies.* Ann Arbor, MI: Open Humanities Press, 2012.

Driel, Edwin van. "Schleiermacher's Supralapsarian Christology." *Scottish Journal of Theology* 60, no. 3 (2007): 251–70.

Elgendy, Rick. "Reconsidering Resurrection, Incarnation, and Nature in Schleiermacher's *Glaubenslehre*." *International Journal of Systematic Theology* 15, no. 3 (2013): 301–23.

Episcopal Church. "Environmental Issues and the Anglican Communion." Video. Last modified April 13, 2016. https://www.episcopalchurch.org/library/video/environmental-issues-and-anglican-communion.

Evans, Christopher. *Liberalism without Illusions: Renewing an American Christian Tradition.* Waco, TX: Baylor University Press, 2010.

Evans, Susan, and Mary Minette. "Hunger and Climate Change: Agriculture and Food Security in a Changing Climate." Evangelical Lutheran Church in America, 2010. goo.gl/aqnuLg.

Fergusson, David. "Predestination: A Scottish Perspective." *Scottish Journal of Theology* 46, no. 4 (1993): 479–96.

Ferris, Elizabeth. "Natural Disaster and Conflict-Induced Displacement: Similarities, Differences, and Inter-Connections." In *Environmental Protection and Human Rights,* edited by Donald K. Anton and Dinah L. Shelton. New York: Cambridge University Press, 2011.

Fiorenza, Elisabeth Schüssler. *Wisdom Ways: Introducing Feminist Biblical Interpretation.* Maryknoll, NY: Orbis Books, 2001.

Fox, Matthew. *The Coming of the Cosmic Christ: The Healing of Mother Earth and the Birth of a Global Renaissance.* San Francisco: Harper & Row, 1988.

———. *Original Blessing.* New York: Tarcher Perigee, 2000.

Francis, Pope. *Laudato Si': On Care for Our Common Home.* Huntington, IN: Our Sunday Visitor, 2015.

Galgani, François, Georg Hanke, and Thomas Maes. "Global Distribution, Composition and Abundance of Marine Litter." In Bergmann, Gutow, and Klages, *Marine Anthropogenic Litter,* 29–56.

Galloway, Tamara S. "Micro- and Nano-plastics and Human Health." In Bergmann, Gutow, and Klages, *Marine Anthropogenic Litter,* 343–66.

Gerrish, Brian A. *Christian Faith: Dogmatics in Outline.* Louisville, KY: Westminster John Knox Press, 2015.

———. *Continuing the Reformation: Essays on Modern Religious Thought.* Chicago: University of Chicago Press, 1993.

———. *A Prince of the Church: Schleiermacher and the Beginnings of Modern Theology.* Eugene, OR: Wipf & Stock, 2001.

———. *Tradition and the Modern World: Reformed Theology in the Nineteenth Century.* Chicago: University of Chicago Press, 1978.

Ghiloni, Aaron J. *John Dewey among the Theologians.* New York: Peter Lang, 2012.

Gockel, Matthias. *Barth and Schleiermacher on the Doctrine of Election: A Systematic-Theological Comparison.* New York: Oxford University Press, 2006.

Greenpeace. "The E-Waste Problem." Accessed May 2016. http://www.green peace.org/international/en/campaigns/detox/electronics/the-e-waste -problem/.

Griffin, David Ray, ed. *Spirituality and Society: Postmodern Visions.* Albany: State University of New York Press, 1988.

Gunton, Colin E. *Christ and Creation.* Carlisle, UK: Paternoster Press, 1992.

———. "The Doctrine of Creation." In *Cambridge Companion to Christian Doctrine,* edited by Colin Gunton, 141–57. Cambridge: Cambridge University Press, 1997.

———. "Election and Ecclesiology in the Post-Constantinian Church." *Scottish Journal of Theology* 53, no. 2 (2000): 212–27.

———. *The One, the Three, and the Many: God, Creation, and the Culture of Modernity.* New York: Cambridge University Press, 1993.

Gutiérrez, Gustavo. *A Theology of Liberation: History, Politics, and Salvation.* Translated and edited by Sr. Caridad Inda and John Eagleson. Maryknoll, NY: Orbis Books, 1986.

Hagan, Anette I. *Eternal Blessedness for All? A Historical-Systematic Examination of Friedrich Schleiermacher's Reinterpretation of Predestination.* Eugene, OR: Pickwick Publications, 2013.

Haight, Roger, SJ. *Christian Community in History.* Vol. 3, *Ecclesial Existence.* New York: Continuum, 2008.

Hart, David B. *The Doors of the Sea*. Grand Rapids: Wm. B. Eerdmans Publishing Co., 2005.

Harvey, Van A. "A Word in Defense of Schleiermacher's Theological Method." *Journal of Religion* 42, no. 3 (1962): 151–70.

Hasler, Ueli. *Beherrschte Natur: Die Anpassung der Theologie an die bürgerliche Naturauffassung im 19. Jahrhundert (Schleiermacher, Ritschl, Herrmann)*. Bern: Peter Lang, 1982.

Hebblethwaite, B. L. "Some Reflections on Predestination, Providence and Divine Foreknowledge." *Religious Studies* 15, no. 4 (1979): 433–48.

Hector, Kevin. "Actualism and Incarnation: The High Christology of Friedrich Schleiermacher." *International Journal of Systematic Theology* 8, no. 3 (July 2006): 307–22.

———. *Theology without Metaphysics: God, Language, and the Spirit of Recognition*. Cambridge: Cambridge University Press, 2011.

Heinegg, Peter. "The Ecological Curse: A Reading of Genesis 3." *CrossCurrents* 65, no. 4 (December 2015): 441–47.

Helmer, Christine. *Theology and the End of Doctrine*. Louisville, KY: Westminster John Knox Press, 2014.

Herms, Eilert. "Reich Gottes und menschliches Handeln." In *Friedrich Schleiermacher 1768–1834: Theologe, Philosoph, Pädagoge*, edited by Dietz Lange, 163–92. Göttingen: Vandenhoeck & Ruprecht, 1985.

———. "Schleiermachers Eschatologie." *Theologische Zeitschrift* 46 (1990): 97–123.

———. "Schleiermachers Eschatologie nach der zweiten Auflage der Glaubenslehre." In *Menschsein im Werden: Studien zu Schleiermacher*, 125–49. Tübingen: Mohr Siebeck, 2003.

Hessel, Dieter T., ed. *After Nature's Revolt: Eco-Justice and Theology*. Minneapolis: Fortress Press, 1992.

———, ed. *Theology for Earth Community: A Field Guide*. Maryknoll, NY: Orbis Books, 1996.

Hessel, Dieter T., and Rosemary Radford Ruether, eds. *Christianity and Ecology: Seeking the Well-Being of the Earth and Humans*. Religions of the World and Ecology 3. Cambridge, MA: Harvard University Press, 2000.

Hieb, Nathan D. "The Precarious State of Resurrection in Friedrich Schleiermacher's *Glaubenslehre*." *International Journal of Systematic Theology* 9, no. 4 (2007): 398–414.

Hurt, R. Douglas. *The Dust Bowl: An Agricultural and Social History*. Chicago: Nelson Hall, 1981.

Johnson, Elizabeth A. *She Who Is: The Mystery of God in Feminist Theological Discourse*. 10th anniv. ed. New York: Crossroad Publishing, 2002.

Jungkeit, Stephen R. *Spaces of Modern Theology: Geography and Power in Schleiermacher's World*. New York: Palgrave Macmillan, 2012.

Kant, Immanuel. *Critique of the Power of Judgment*. Edited by Paul Guyer. Translated by Paul Guyer and Eric Matthews. Cambridge: Cambridge University Press, 2000.

———. *Critique of Practical Reason*. Translated by Lewis White Beck. Indianapolis: Bobbs-Merrill Educational Publishing, 1956.

———. *Metaphysical Foundations of Natural Science*. Translated and edited by Michael Friedman. Cambridge: Cambridge University Press, 2004.

Kelsey, Catherine L. *Thinking about Christ with Schleiermacher*. Louisville, KY: Westminster John Knox Press, 2003.

Kim, Sung-Sup. *Deus Providebit: Calvin, Schleiermacher, and Barth on the Providence of God*. Emerging Scholars Series. Minneapolis: Fortress Press, 2014.

Kingsolver, Barbara. Foreword to *Thoreau's Legacy: American Stories about Global Warming*, edited by Richard Hayes, 7–9. Cambridge, MA: Union of Concerned Scientists, 2009.

Klein, Naomi. *No Is Not Enough: Resisting Trump's Shock Politics and Winning the World We Need*. Chicago: Haymarket Books, 2017.

———. *This Changes Everything: Capitalism vs. the Climate*. New York: Simon & Schuster, 2014.

Kühn, Susanne, Elisa L. Bravo Rebolledo, and Jan A. van Graneker. "Deleterious Effects of Litter on Marine Life." In Bergmann, Gutow, and Klages, *Marine Anthropogenic Litter*, 75–116.

Kunnuthara, Abraham Varghese. *Schleiermacher on Christian Consciousness of God's Work in History*. Princeton Theological Monograph Series 76. Eugene, OR: Pickwick Publications, 2008.

Lamm, Julia. *The Living God: Schleiermacher's Theological Appropriation of Spinoza*. University Park: Pennsylvania State University Press, 1996.

Lay, Thorne, Hiroo Kanamori, Charles J. Ammon, Meredith Nettles, Steven N. Ward, Richard C. Aster, Susan L. Beck, Susan L. Bilek, Michael R. Brudzinski, Rhett Butler, Heather R. DeShon, Göran Ekström, Kenji Satake, and Stuart Sipkin. "The Great Sumatra-Andaman Earthquake of 26 December 2004." *Science* 308, no. 5725 (May 20, 2005): 1127–33.

Libecap, Gary D., and Zeynep Kocabiyik Hansen. "'Rain Follows the Plow' and Dryfarming Doctrine: The Climate Information Problem and Homestead Failure in the Upper Great Plains, 1890–1925." *Journal of Economic History* 62, no. 1 (2002): 86–120.

Lindbeck, George. *The Nature of Doctrine: Religion and Theology in a Postliberal Age*. Louisville, KY: Westminster/John Knox Press, 1984.

Lookingbill, Brad D. *Dust Bowl, USA: Depression America and the Ecological Imagination, 1929–1941*. Athens: Ohio University Press, 2001.

Lucas, J. R. "Foreknowledge." In *Philosophy in Christianity*, edited by G. Vesey, 122. Cambridge: Cambridge University Press, 1989.

MacDonald, Rhona. "How Women Were Affected by the Tsunami: A Perspective from Oxfam." *PLoS Medicine* 2, no. 6 (June 28, 2005): doi:10.1371/journal.pmed.0020178.

Mackintosh, Hugh Ross. *Types of Modern Theology: Schleiermacher to Barth*. London: Nisbet and Co., 1937.

Mariña, Jaqueline. *Transformation of the Self in the Thought of Friedrich Schleiermacher*. Oxford: Oxford University Press, 2008.

Mayer, Jane. *Dark Money: The Hidden History of the Billionaires behind the Rise of the Radical Right*. New York: Doubleday, 2016.

McFague, Sallie. "God's Household: Christianity, Economics, and Planetary Living." In *Subverting Greed: Religious Perspectives in the Global Economy*, edited by Paul F. Knitter and Chandra Muzaffar, 119–36. Maryknoll, NY: Orbis Books, 2002.

———. *Life Abundant: Rethinking Theology and Economy for a Planet in Peril.* Minneapolis: Fortress Press, 2001.

———. *Models of God: Theology for an Ecological, Nuclear Age.* Minneapolis: Fortress Press, 1987.

McKibben, Bill. *The End of Nature.* New York: Random House, 1989. Reissued 2006.

Moltmann, Jürgen. *God in Creation: A New Theology of Creation and the Spirit of God.* Translated by Margaret Kohl. San Francisco: Harper & Row, 1985.

Moore, Charles J. "Choking the Oceans with Plastic." *New York Times*, August 25, 2014. http://www.nytimes.com/2014/08/26/opinion/choking-the -oceans-with-plastic.html?ref=opinion&_r=3.

Moore, Charles J., and Cassandra Phillips. *Plastic Oceans: How a Sea Captain's Chance Discovery Launched a Determined Quest to Save the Oceans.* New York: Penguin Press, 2011.

Mueller, Wolfgang Erich. Introduction to *Die christliche Sitte nach den Grundsätzen der evangelischen Kirche im Zusammenhang dargestellt,* by Friedrich Schleiermacher. Theologische Studien-Texte 7.1. Waltrop: Spenner, 1999.

Nelson, Derek R. *What's Wrong with Sin? Sin in Individual and Social Perspective from Schleiermacher to Theologies of Liberation.* Edinburgh: T&T Clark, 2009.

Niebuhr, Reinhold. *The Nature and Destiny of Man.* Vol. 1. Louisville, KY: Westminster John Knox Press, 1996.

Niebuhr, Richard R. *Schleiermacher on Christ and Religion.* New York: Charles Scribner's Sons, 1964.

Nimmo, Paul. "Schleiermacher on Justification: A Departure from the Reformation?" *Scottish Journal of Theology* 66, no. 1 (2013): 50–73.

———. "Schleiermacher on Scripture and the Work of Jesus Christ." *Modern Theology* 31, no. 1 (January 2015): 60–90.

Norgaard, Kari Marie. *Living in Denial: Climate Change, Emotions, and Everyday Life.* Cambridge, MA: MIT Press, 2011.

Oberdorfer, Bernd. "Schleiermacher on Eschatology and Resurrection." In *Resurrection: Theological and Scientific Assessments,* edited by Ted Peters, Robert J. Russell, and Michael Welker, 165–82. Grand Rapids: Wm. B. Eerdmans Publishing Co., 2002.

Oliver, Mary. *Felicity.* New York: Penguin Press, 2016.

———. *New and Selected Poems.* 2 vols. Boston: Beacon Press, 1992–2005.

Pedersen, Daniel. "Eternal Life in Schleiermacher's *The Christian Faith.*" *International Journal of Systematic Theology* 13, no. 3 (2011): 340–57.

Pfister, Thomas, Martin Schweighofer, and André Reichel. *Sustainability.* New York: Routledge, 2016.

Poe, M. Shelli. *Essential Trinitarianism: Schleiermacher as Trinitarian Theologian.* T&T Clark Explorations in Reformed Theology. New York: Bloomsbury Publishing, 2017.

———. "Friedrich Schleiermacher's Theology as a Resource for Ecological Economics." *Theology Today* 73, no. 1 (2016): 9–23.

Pollin, Robert. *Greening the Global Economy.* Cambridge, MA: MIT Press, 2015.

Portney, Kent E. *Sustainability.* Cambridge, MA: MIT Press, 2015.

Presbyterian Church (U.S.A.) Advisory Committee on Social Witness Policy. "The Power to Change: U.S. Energy Policy and Global Warming." 2008. https://www.presbyterianmission.org.

Purdy, Jedediah. *After Nature: A Politics for the Anthropocene*. Cambridge, MA: Harvard University Press, 2015.

Rahner, Karl. *The Foundations of Christian Faith: An Introduction to the Idea of Christianity*. Translated by William V. Dych. New York: Crossroad Publishing, 1982.

———. *The Trinity*. Translated by Joseph Donceel. New York: Crossroad Publishing, 1997.

Rasmussen, Larry L. *Earth Community, Earth Ethics*. Maryknoll, NY: Orbis Books, 1996.

———. Epilogue to *Theology for Earth Community: A Field Guide*, edited by Dieter T. Hessel, 265–68. Maryknoll, NY: Orbis Books, 1996.

Rauschenbusch, Walter. *Theology for the Social Gospel*. Louisville, KY: Westminster John Knox Press, 1997.

Redeker, Martin. Introduction to *Der christliche Glaube nach den Grundsätzen der evangelischen Kirche im Zusammenhange dargestellt*, edited by Martin Redeker. 2 vols. 7th ed., based on 2nd ed. of 1830–31, xiii–xl. Berlin: Walter de Gruyter, 1960.

Reynolds, Thomas. "Reconsidering Schleiermacher and the Problem of Religious Diversity." *Journal of the American Academy of Religion* 73, no. 1 (2005): 151–81.

Rieger, Joerg. *Christ and Empire*. Minneapolis: Fortress Press, 2007.

Root, Michael. "Schleiermacher as Innovator and Inheritor: God, Dependence and Election." *Scottish Journal of Theology* 43, no. 1 (1990): 87–110.

Ruether, Rosemary Radford. *Gaia and God: An Ecofeminist Theology of Earth Healing*. New York: HarperCollins, 1992.

———. *Integrating Ecofeminism, Globalization, and World Religions*. New York: Rowman & Littlefield, 2005.

———. *Sexism and God-Talk: Toward a Feminist Theology*. Boston: Beacon Press, 1983.

Ryan, Peter G., Charles J. Moore, Jan A. van Franeker, and Coleen L. Moloney. "Monitoring the Abundance of Plastic Debris in the Marine Environment." *Philosophical Transactions of the Royal Society B: Biological Sciences* 364, no. 1526 (2009): 1999–2012.

Santmire, H. Paul. "Ecotheology." In *Encyclopedia of Science and Religion*, Vol. 1, A–I, edited by J. Wentzel Vrede van Huyssteen, 247–51. New York: Macmillan Reference USA, 2003.

Schleiermacher, Friedrich. *Aus Schleiermachers Leben, In Briefen*. Edited by L. Jonas and W. Dilthey. 4 vols. Berlin, 1858–63.

———. *Brief Outline of the Study of Theology*. Translated by William Farrer. Reprint, Eugene, OR: Wipf & Stock, 1850.

———. *Brief Outline of Theology as a Field of Study*. 3rd ed. Louisville, KY: Westminster John Knox Press, 2011.

———. *Christian Caring: Selections from* Practical Theology. Edited and with an introduction by James O. Duke and Howard Stone. Translated by James O. Duke. Philadelphia: Fortress Press, 1988.

————. *The Christian Faith*. Edited by H. R. Mackintosh and J. S. Stewart. New York: T&T Clark, 1999.

————. *Christian Faith: A New Translation and Critical Edition*. Translated by Terrence N. Tice, Catherine L. Kelsey, and Edwina Lawler. Edited by Catherine L. Kelsey and Terrence N. Tice. 2 vols. Louisville, KY: Westminster John Knox Press, 2016.

————. "Christ Is Like Us in All Things but Sin." In *Schleiermacher: Christmas Dialogue, The Second Speech, and Other Selections*, edited and translated by Julia A. Lamm, 241–49. New York: Paulist Press, 2014.

————. *Der christliche Glaube nach den Grundsätzen der evangelischen Kirche im Zusammenhange dargestellt*. 7th ed., based on 2nd ed. of 1830–31. Edited by Martin Redeker. 2 vols. Berlin: Walter de Gruyter, 1960.

————. *Der christliche Glaube nach den Grundsätzen der evangelischen Kirche im Zusammenhange dargestellt, Zweite Auflage (1830/31)*. Edited by Rolf Schäfer. *Kritische Gesamtausgabe (KGA)* I.13.1. Berlin: Walter de Gruyter, 2003.

————. *Die christliche Sitte nach den Grundsätzen der evangelischen Kirche im Zusammenhange dargestellt*. Edited by Ludwig Jonas. *Sämmtliche Werke* I.12. Berlin: G. Reimer, 1843. Reprint, Waltrop: Verlag Hartmut Spenner, 1999.

————. *Christliche Sittenlehre (Vorlesung im Wintersemester 1826/27). Nach größtenteils unveröffentlichten Hörernachschriften und nach teilweise unveröffentlichten Manuskripten Schleiermachers*. Edited by Hermann Peiter. Berlin: LIT Verlag, 2010.

————. *Dialectic; or, The Art of Doing Philosophy: A Study Edition of the 1811 Notes*. Translated by Terrence N. Tice. Atlanta: Scholars Press, 1996.

————. *Dialektik* (1822). Band 2. Edited by Manfred Frank. Berlin: Suhrkamp Verlag, 2001.

————. *Friedrich Schleiermachers sämmtliche Werke, Dritte Abtheilung. Zur Philosophie. Sechster Band*, III.6, *Psychologie*. Edited by L. George. Berlin: G. Reimer, 1862.

————. *Kritische Gesamtausgabe*. Abt. I, Bd. 11, *Akademievorträge*. Edited by Martin Rößler. Berlin: de Gruyter, 2002.

————. *Kritische Gesamtausgabe*. Abt. II, Bd. 10, t. 1, *Vorlesungen über die Dialektik*. Edited by Andreas Arndt. Berlin: de Gruyter, 2002.

————. *Lectures on Philosophical Ethics*. Edited by Robert B. Louden. Translated by Louise Adey Huish. Cambridge: Cambridge University Press, 2002.

————. *On the Doctrine of Election, with Special Reference to the Aphorisms of Dr. Bretschneider*. Translated by Iain G. Nicol and Allen G. Jorgenson. Columbia Series in Reformed Theology. Louisville, KY: Westminster John Knox Press, 2006.

————. *On the* Glaubenslehre. Translated by James Duke and Francis Fiorenza. Atlanta: Scholars Press, 1981.

————. *On Religion: Speeches to Its Cultured Despisers*. Translated and edited by Richard Crouter. New York: Cambridge University Press, 1996.

————. *Pädagogik: Die Theorie der Erziehung von 1820/21 in einer Nachschrift*. Edited by Christiane Ehrhardt and Wolfgang Virmond. Berlin: de Gruyter, 2008.

―――. *Schleiermacher: Christmas Dialogue, The Second Speech, and Other Selections*. Edited and translated by Julia A. Lamm. New York: Paulist Press, 2014.

―――. *Schleiermachers Vorlesungen über die Aesthetik vorgetragen Ao. 1832– 1833*. Nachlass Alexander Schweizer. Available on the Schleiermacher in Berlin 1808–1834 project website, http://schleiermacher-in-berlin.bbaw .de/vorlesungen/detail.xql?id=prov_shf_hbq_2r.

―――. *Selections from Friedrich Schleiermacher's* Christian Ethics. Edited and translated by James M. Brandt. Louisville, KY: Westminster John Knox Press, 2011.

―――. *Servant of the Word: Selected Sermons of Friedrich Schleiermacher*. Translated by Dawn DeVries. Philadelphia: Fortress Press, 1987.

―――. "Über den Begriff des höchsten Gutes. Zweite Abhandlung." *KGA* I.11, 657–78.

―――. "Über den Unterschied zwischen Naturgesetz und Sittengesetz." *KGA* I.11, 429–52.

―――. *"Über die Begriffe der verschiedenen Staatsformen." KGA* I.11, 95–124.

Schwanke, Johannes. "Martin Luther's Doctrine of Creation." In *Oxford Research Encyclopedia of Religion*. Published online March 2017. doi:10.1093 /acrefore/9780199340378.013.329.

Schwöbel, Christoph. "Divine Agency and Providence." *Modern Theology* 3, no. 3 (1987): 225–44.

Sherman, Robert. *The Shift to Modernity: Christ and the Doctrine of Creation in the Theologies of Schleiermacher and Barth*. New York: T&T Clark, 2005.

Sockness, Brent W., and Wilhelm Gräb, eds. *Schleiermacher, the Study of Religion, and the Future of Theology: A Transatlantic Dialogue*. Berlin: Walter de Gruyter, 2010.

Steinbeck, John. *The Grapes of Wrath*. New York: Viking Press, 1939.

Süskind, Herman. *Der Einfluss Schellings auf die Entwicklung von Schleiermachers System*. Tübingen: J. C. B. Mohr, 1909.

Sydnor, Jon Paul. *Ramanuja and Schleiermacher: Toward a Constructive Comparative Theology*. Cambridge: James Clarke & Co., 2012.

Tanner, Kathryn. *Economy of Grace*. Minneapolis: Fortress Press, 2005.

Thandeka. *The Embodied Self: Friedrich Schleiermacher's Solution to Kant's Problem of the Empirical Self*. Albany: State University of New York Press, 1995.

Theokritoff, Elizabeth. *Living in God's Creation: Orthodox Perspectives on Ecology*. Crestwood, NY: St. Vladimir's Seminary Press, 2009.

Tice, Terrence N. Introduction to *Dialectic; or, The Art of Doing Philosophy*, by Friedrich Schleiermacher, xi–xxv. Atlanta: Scholars Press, 1996.

―――. *Schleiermacher*. Nashville: Abingdon Press, 2006.

United Church of Christ. "Environmental Racism." http://www.ucc.org /environmental-ministries_environmental-racism.

U.S. Government Accountability Office. "Electronic Waste: EPA Needs to Better Control Harmful U.S. Exports through Stronger Enforcement and More Comprehensive Regulation." August 28, 2008. https://www.gao .gov/products/GAO-08-1044.

Vander Schel, Kevin M. *Embedded Grace: Christ, History, and the Reign of God in Schleiermacher's Dogmatics*. Minneapolis: Fortress Press, 2013.

———. "Friedrich Schleiermacher." In *T&T Clark Companion to the Doctrine of Sin*, edited by Keith L. Johnson and David Lauber. New York: Bloomsbury T&T Clark, 2016.

Vial, Theodore. *Schleiermacher: A Guide for the Perplexed*. London: Bloomsbury T&T Clark, 2013.

Weeber, Martin. *Schleiermachers Eschatologie: Eine Untersuchung zum theologischen Spätwerk*. Gütersloh: Christian Kaiser, 2000.

Welch, Claude. *Protestant Thought in the Nineteenth Century*. 2 vols. New Haven, CT: Yale University Press: 1985.

White, Lynn, Jr. "The Historical Roots of Our Ecological Crisis." *Science* 155, no. 3767 (1967): 1203–7.

Wilcox, Jeffrey A., Terrence N. Tice, and Catherine L. Kelsey, eds. *Schleiermacher's Influences on American Thought and Religious Life, 1835–1920*. 3 vols. Eugene, OR: Wipf & Stock, 2013.

Wyman, Walter E. "Rethinking the Christian Doctrine of Sin: Friedrich Schleiermacher and Hick's 'Irenaean Type.'" *Journal of Religion* 74, no. 2 (1994): 199–217.

INDEX OF NAMES